Sartre's Marxism

By the same author:

Critical Theory of the Family, New York, The Seabury Press; London, Pluto Press 1978

Existential Marxism in Postwar France, Princeton, N.J., Princeton University Press 1975

The Utopian Thought of Restif de la Bretonne, New York, New York University Press 1971

Mark Poster

Sartre's Marxism

Pluto  Press

First published 1979 by Pluto Press Limited
Unit 10 Spencer Court, 7 Chalcot Road, London NW1 8LH
Copyright © Pluto Press 1979
ISBN 0 86104 084 8
Printed and bound in Great Britain at
The Camelot Press Limited, Southampton
Designed by Richard Hollis, GrR

Acknowledgements

A Summer Fellowship from the Regents of the University of California enabled me to complete the major portion of this text in a reasonable time. My dear friend, Jonathan Wiener, studied the manuscript meticulously, offering countless improvements in style and content, which, for the most part, I have heeded. Richard Kuper, of Pluto Press, suggested the idea for this book and worked with me to make it as readable as possible.

For Jamie

Contents

Introduction / 9

1. Reason and Revolution / 17

2. The Limits of Dialectical Reason / 32

3. 'Men and Things' / 49

4. Groups, Organisations and Institutions / 81

5. Conclusions / 112

References / 121

Index / 129

Introduction

Some scepticism might be voiced over the attribution of marxism to the thought of Jean-Paul Sartre. The French thinker remains in some quarters a petty-bourgeois intellectual and in others a respected philosopher of pessimism, despair and anxiety — anything but a prophet of revolution. These decidedly un-marxist images have pursued Sartre long after he aligned himself theoretically with marxism in 1960, eschewing his early position in *Being and Nothingness*. Nevertheless, Sartre's politics have been anything but a linear rush onward towards Marx and communism. Since the resistance, Sartre has been a man of the left; that much consistency must be granted. Within this position, however, there have been numerous manoeuvrings and shifts in relation both to the thought of Marx and the politics of the French Communist Party. Most recently Sartre has disavowed allegiance both to the party and to the principles of historical materialism.[1] Thus 'Sartre's marxism' must be defined carefully if we are to avoid confusions.

In a sense Sartre has always been a radical. His early existentialist writings, *The Transcendence of the Ego* (1936), *Nausea* (1938) and *Being and Nothingness* (1943), all challenged official liberal culture. The philosophical works undermined the dominant, bourgeois theories of knowledge based on rationalism and positivism. The literary writings were decidedly modernist, opposing the basic assumptions of the classical bourgeois novel. Until the second world war, however, Sartre's thought remained apolitical and did not confront marxism. The experience of the French resistance against fascism changed all that. Sartre the existentialist, confined in a German prisoner of war camp and then living in Nazi-occupied Paris, was compelled to take sides and he chose the left.

From the end of the second world war until the Soviet invasion of Hungary, Sartre adopted various positions with respect to marxism both in his writings and in his politics. During these years marxism was represented in France most visibly by the French Communist Party which maintained close relations with the Soviet Union. In the cold war context Sartre generally sided with the communists against the United States and its allies. The exception came when Sartre joined the neutralist Rassemblement Démocratique Révolutionnaire for a brief period in the late 1940s. The RDR, short-lived and inconsequential, sought a 'third-force' that would lead Europe out of the conundrums of the cold war. Aside from that interlude Sartre was clearly identified with the pro-communist camp.

Sartre's adherence to the Soviet position must not be overemphasised. Unhappy with capitalism and liberal democracy, Sartre was by no means a spokesman for the proletariat, much less for stalinism. In support of popular, democratic movements, Sartre remained independent of the CP and suspicious of marxism's claim as sole representative of the oppressed. When protest movements or revolts broke out in French colonies such as Vietnam and Algeria Sartre was quick to support the anti-imperialist forces – often much quicker than the French Communist Party and sometimes in contradiction with it. The thread that runs with consistency through Sartre's political history, from 1945 to the present, is an independent radicalism that sides with the oppressed against the powerful. In the recent affair in which the farmers of Larzac resisted the efforts of the French army to convert their land into a military base Sartre struggled with the people.

Have Sartre's politics been marxist or merely adventurist, as the French communists have often claimed? The underlying question concerns the role of the intellectual: must a marxist, be he an intellectual or not, join the dominant workers' party or can he function independently? In several interviews in the 1970s[2] Sartre reflected on his development, characterising his early career as that of a classical intellectual leftist who had become, or sought to become, a friend of the people, a leftist intellectual. In other words Sartre views himself as an independent intellectual who has aligned himself with the people and who struggles with the oppressed wherever that struggle leads. Thus Sartre defines himself as one committed to the oppressed and available for political work. The fate of the leftist intellectual is tied closely to that of the people.

These observations on the role of the intellectual do not resolve the question of Sartre's marxism. They reveal only his firm conviction that the intellectual must be free of manipulation by the party, free to exercise his critical judgment and free to criticise the party itself. From 1945 to 1957 Sartre did just that. He wrote numerous essays on politics, literature and marxist theory in which he tried to come to terms with the theory and practice of marxism. Sartre's path to marxism, however, was encumbered by several difficult obstacles. The first was the Soviet Union itself, the living embodiment of marxism which was blemished by purge trials, labour camps, political repression and an authoritarian state. The second was the French Communist Party which slavishly followed the dictates of the Soviet Union instead of developing marxist theory into a viable path for socialism in France. The third was the rigidity of marxist theory which, at the hands of Stalin, had become an official doctrine, not a heuristic, critical theory. Sartre's writings from 1945 to 1957 may be seen as an effort to find the revolutionary kernel of marxism within its stalinist husk.

At the end of the war Sartre, along with his friends Simone de Beauvoir and Maurice Merleau-Ponty, established *Les Temps Modernes* as the base for his search for a viable marxism. *What Is Literature?* was the first essay to emerge from this period. Against the prevailing view of literature as beyond politics and against the stalinist reduction of literature to politics, Sartre enunciated a theory of the committed writer. Already in *What Is Literature?* Sartre was developing the groundwork for his radicalism. His hesitations about marxism, however, were made public about the same time in his essay 'Materialism and Revolution' (1946). Here Sartre explored the contradiction within a stalinist marxism that advocated revolution yet depicted history as determined by objective laws. A revolutionary philosophy, Sartre contended, must capture humanity as the free creators of society. One could not at the same time pontificate about a workers' revolution and view history as the outcome of mechanical laws. Thus before Sartre could become a marxist he would have to abandon its stalinist form and discover within the writings of Marx and Engels a theory in which man made history. Sartre needed to discover how the class struggle operated, specifically how the contemporary working class could be understood as the agent of history, as the free, revolutionary group that could give birth to socialist society.

In *Being and Nothingness* Sartre had given prominence to freedom in the human condition. Humanity was free to make itself, Sartre had argued, and no force, natural, social or supernatural, could thwart that freedom. Radical as it was, the doctrine of freedom in *Being and Nothingness* was a far cry from marxism. Human freedom was not situated historically and socially, but applied equally to fascists and communists, to a sixteenth-century monk and a nineteenth-century factory worker. Because of this, the concept of freedom in *Being and Nothingness* appeared to be idealist, concerned with how individuals in isolation created their own values, not with concrete social subjects. After 1943, when Sartre became active in politics, he sought to reconcile his concept of freedom with a marxist concept of society.

Sartre's friend, Merleau-Ponty, played an important role in this transition. Merleau-Ponty had been the political editor for *Les Temps Modernes* and was more informed about marxism and social questions than Sartre. His writings in the late 1940s and early 1950s, collected in *Sense and Non-Sense* (1948) and *Signs* (1960), pioneered the path towards a synthesis of existentialism and marxism. In *Humanism and Terror* (1947) Merleau-Ponty attacked the liberal view of the Soviet purge trials and defended the violence that accompanied socialist revolutions. By the time of the Korean war, in 1952, Merleau-Ponty had lost hope in the working class as the agent of an emancipatory politics and *Adventures of the Dialectic*

(1955) dismissed any attempt to defend marxism or to reconcile it with existentialism.

In 1952 Sartre's views were quite different. In that year *The Communists and the Peace* appeared. Now Sartre was not only defending marxism but was giving his full support to the policies of the French Communist Party. *The Communists and the Peace* was a fiery polemic against capitalism and the politics of the fourth republic. Sartre argued that only the working class could advance the cause of human freedom:

> In France today, only the working class is equipped with a doctrine. It is the only class whose particular interests are the interests of the nation. A great party represents them, the only one to have made it part of its program to safeguard democratic institutions, reestablish national sovereignty and defend the peace, the only one to concern itself with democratic rebirth and the increase of buying power; the only one, finally, that is *alive*, that literally crawls with life while the others crawl with worms.[3]

Sartre's discovery of marxism and the French Communist Party certainly arrived with a vengeance. After 1952 Sartre developed his marxism in greater depth, but he never again gave such strong support to the party.

Indeed, *The Ghost of Stalin*, written in response to the Soviet invasion of Hungary in 1956, revealed Sartre as a formidable opponent of the French Communist Party and of stalinism in general. In the space of four years Sartre's understanding of politics had matured considerably. The existentialist now separated the emancipatory potential of the proletariat, and all oppressed groups, from the leadership of the Soviet Union and its satellite parties in Europe. Although Sartre in *The Ghost of Stalin* renounced communism he did not give up on marxism. In fact, his marxism took a giant step forward. For in this essay Sartre seriously began the business of developing the concepts that would reconcile the concept of freedom in *Being and Nothingness* with the social doctrine of historical materialism. He presented a penetrating analysis of the role of the Soviet Union in Eastern European politics which acknowledged the role of the situation – social forces, the economy, political alliances – in the play of individual freedom. No longer could Sartre write about human freedom at the purely ontological level, as if it existed for everyone at all times in exactly the same way. From now on the existentialist sense of freedom would have to be rooted in history. And the interpretation of history that Sartre adopted was that of Marx.

Although *The Ghost of Stalin* marked an important stage in Sartre's odyssey towards marxism and is interesting in its own right as a piece of political analysis, the main task of originating a critical marxism remained for the future. In 1957 Sartre wrote *Search For a Method* and in 1960 the full text of volume one of the *Critique of Dialectical Reason* appeared. Only in these writings does Sartre's social theory emerge fully. The *Critique*, which included *Search For a Method* as its preface, presents a thorough rethinking of marxist social theory and a systematic effort to integrate the valuable parts of existentialism into marxism. Yet in the English-speaking world Sartre's contribution to marxism has barely been recognised. He remains either an existentialist or an erratic radical who refused to accept the Nobel Prize for Literature and who sold radical newspapers in the streets of Paris. The important theoretical advances of the *Critique* have remained in obscurity. Part of the blame rests with Sartre for the *Critique* is extremely difficult to read. It is simply inaccessible to most readers, even to those informed about marxism and social theory. There is a need then for a systematic treatment of the *Critique* from a sympathetic point of view which evaluates its contribution to emancipatory social theory.

When the *Critique* appeared in Paris in 1960 the political situation had altered considerably from the cold war period. The alternative was no longer that of supporting uncritically the French Communist Party or risking betrayal to the imperialist camp. The Hungarian invasion had demonstrated the weakness of stalinism. In addition the CP in France was slow to support the struggle for independence in Algeria, no doubt because Russia wanted no challenge from communists to the bourgeois democracies. Furthermore, the 20th Congress of the Soviet Communist Party had denounced the excesses of Stalin, throwing into confusion all those who unconditionally supported the communist homeland. Economically, too, gaullist France was headed for a new period of modernisation and growth. Given these new conditions the search for an independent marxism, which had previously been the project of a few ex-trotskyists and isolated intellectuals in France, became the order of the day. The time was ripe for a new left and Sartre's *Critique* was an important example of the new direction.

From the point of view of marxist social theory, Sartre's *Critique of Dialectical Reason* presents a challenge and an opening for new lines of development. This book will be concerned solely with Sartre's *Critique* and it will explore the extent to which marxist theory can benefit from it. The problematic here pursued is that the traditional categories of historical materialism cannot account for (1) changes from classical to advanced capitalist society and (2) certain features of pre-capitalist modes of production. Sartre's *Critique* helps overcome theoretical deficiencies within the works of Marx and Engels concerning the adequacy of their positions for a critical social theory, deficiencies which bear directly on the ability of marxism to account for historic developments of the twentieth century.

The position maintained in this book — as well as by Sartre in the *Critique* — is that the deficiencies enumerated and the revisions suggested do not constitute a rejection of marxism but an enrichment of it. Perhaps neo-marxism is the best designation for Sartre's theory. In any case, the general strategy of the *Critique* may be grouped with that of other recent social theorists. Sartre is part of the tradition of 'Western marxism' which stretches back to Antonio Gramsci, George Lukacs and Ernst Bloch and continues with the Frankfurt School in Germany, Maurice Merleau-Ponty and even Louis Althusser in France, and many others from all parts of Europe. Some of the positions of individuals in this group are incompatible with that of others; yet they all raise the same cluster of theoretical and political questions. Without intending to diminish the role of other Western

15

marxists for a reconstituted critical theory, I argue that Sartre's contribution is of fundamental importance.

In what follows the procedure is entirely critical and systematic. Sartre's concepts will be summarised only to the extent necessary for an understanding of the issues raised. The limits of space prevent me from tracing the intellectual lineages of the ideas, from putting them in the context of Sartre's earlier and later positions or in the context of Western marxism generally, and from explaining the ideas in relation to the social context.[4] My intentions are critical and temptations to historicise the theory will be avoided. Yet the purpose of the book is eminently historical: to clarify the theoretical problems of Sartre's marxism and thereby provide the basis for a more comprehensive and more self-conscious understanding of history.

1. Reason and Revolution

In *Search For a Method*, an essay written in 1957 and republished together with the original edition of the *Critique of Dialectical Reason* in 1960, Sartre announced that marxism was 'the one philosophy of our time which we cannot go beyond'.[1] The existentialist pledged himself to marxism because the theory of marxism was bound up with the history of our age. Implicit in Sartre's conversion to marxism was an acceptance of a main tenet of historical materialism: that reason is tied up with history. The social philosopher was not to search for eternal truths, universal postulates or absolute maxims. History was both the matrix and horizon of theory. Knowledge was relative to the temporal position of the knower and the situation provided the initiative, the impulse and the exigency of thought.

Sartre could name only three 'moments' of philosophical creation in the past 300 years: Descartes and Locke; Kant and Hegel; and, finally, Marx. These philosophers theorised the limits of knowledge for their time. 'These three philosophies become, each in its turn, the humus of every particular thought and the horizon of all culture; there is no going beyond them so long as man has not gone beyond the historical moment which they express'.[2] The philosopher thus 'expresses' the idea of the age. In this justification of Marx Sartre relies upon a hegelian notion of an expressive totality: philosophy becomes a *Zeitgeist*, a spirit of the time which, nourished in an historical epoch, rises from its soil like a flower giving shape and character to the surrounding landscape while epitomising its very features.[3] The chief problem with Sartre's formulation of the relation of marxism to modernity, as Althusser has pointed out,[4] stems from the reliance upon a notion of a homogeneous totality which contains but a single essence or character expressed within a philosophy. In this sense, the late sixteenth and early seventeenth century was a 'baroque' age in which heteronomous levels like politics, economics, art and religion all exuded the same spirit. Similarly, in the contemporary period, Marx had, for Sartre, somehow captured in his thought the fleeting reality of history.

A weakness in Sartre's marxism was that he nowhere explained precisely the reasons for the insurpassability of historical materialism. The *Critique* provided no discussion of the theory of the mode of production, no examination of the tendencies of capitalist society as outlined in *Capital*, no systematic presentation of historical materialism. Sartre simply asserted the validity of Marx's thought and proclaimed it the theory of the age. Competing systems of thought, such as liberalism or anarchism, were not even mentioned. This dogmatism exists in striking contrast to the main plea of Sartre's position: the call for open, heuristic theory, for unrelenting criticism of all orthodoxies and conventional wisdoms.

Once the credentials of marxism were acknowledged, however, Sartre proceeded ruthlessly to demolish existing versions of historical materialism. Paradoxically, the same marxism that merited the designation of philosophy of the age was also lifeless, sclerotic, arrested in its development. The true, original, real marxism of Marx's text was one thing; the current versions of marxism were quite another. One could quote Marx denouncing the marxists to find scriptural authority for such a duality. Yet Sartre's rejection of stalinism and other forms of marxism current in France was considerably stronger than the father of socialism's blandishments to his superficial sons. For Sartre marxism was at one and the same time the only important intellectual resource of modernity and completely unrepresented by meritorious exponents. One might surmise that Sartre was polemicising for his own theory, pushing aside other versions of marxism to make place for the *Critique*.

According to Sartre's analysis marxism was no longer a vital theory but a rigid orthodoxy devoted to the defence of the Soviet Union:

Marxism stopped. Precisely because this philosophy wants to change the world . . . there arose within it a veritable schism which rejected theory on one side and *praxis* on the other. From the moment the USSR, encircled and alone, undertook its gigantic effort at industrialisation, marxism found itself unable to bear the shock of these new struggles, the practical necessities and the mistakes which are always inseparable from them. At this period of withdrawal (for the USSR) and of ebb tide (for the revolutionary proletariats), the ideology itself was subordinated to a double need: security (that is, unity) and the construction of socialism *inside* the USSR.[5]

The consequences of the Soviet situation were disastrous for marxist theory. Stalin, opposed to open intellectual ferment, imposed a closed dogma on world communism in which marxism was reduced to a simple theory of economic reductionism. From this point on marxist writers were no longer able to account for the ongoing course of history, presenting instead caricatures of the class struggle. Sartre viewed marxist writing as the application of a wooden formula in which the proletariat was always presented as unified under the party for militant revolutionary action, when in fact this was not so.

Tendencies in the direction of mechanical materialism existed before Stalin. Sartre denounced Engels's version of the dialectic of nature[6] as the theoretical heart of the problem. The attempt to discover a dialectic in nature was a false evasion of history in favour of a transcendent law. The dialectic of nature would remove knowledge from its human matrix and give a false, absolute certainty to historical materialism. Human affairs would be reduced to the play of objective forces beyond human control. The contingency of history and the agency of social classes would be eliminated in favour of the inexorable unfolding of an iron necessity. Stalin, Sartre complained, simply regressed to the position of Engels and consigned marxism to the mire of positivism.

Was Sartre's understanding of marxism at this time correct? If marxism were no more than the theory and intellectual work of the stalinists, Sartre's argument was strong. But marxism in 1960 was not limited to the Communist Party. Georges Lefebvre, an independent marxist historian, had written his pathbreaking *Paysans du Nord*; Lucien Goldmann, using the theory of George Lukacs, had published *Le Dieu Caché* in 1956; Henri Lefebvre, a marxist philosopher who left the Party after the Hungarian invasion, had written numerous books of literary criticism and philosophy which escaped the limits of orthodoxy; Pierre Naville, a trotskyist, Daniel Guérin, an anarchist, Cornélius Castoriadis, a libertarian marxist, and numerous others could not be characterised as stalinists. And this list includes only French writers. In Germany, the Frankfurt School, Ernst Bloch and others would have to be considered. Raymond Williams was writing literary criticism in England from a non-stalinist perspective. In the United States, Herbert Marcuse, Paul Baran and Paul Sweezy had all published major works of historical sociology from an independent marxist perspective. Thus, far from being arrested as Sartre thought, marxism was beginning a major revival in the period 1957–60.

If Sartre's claim about the impact of stalinism on marxist writing and theory was exaggerated, he was certainly correct in calling attention to fundamental theoretical problems. Only the insularity of French cultural life could allow him to overlook theoretical openings similar to his own that were emerging throughout Europe and the United States.

The major objection Sartre voiced against most marxist writing was that it could not account for the very thing that was its main objective: that is, revolution. From the onset of socialist theory in Marx's early writings the goal had always been to philosophise history from the point of view of changing the world. Men make history, Marx had written, even though they do so in circumstances they did not choose. The theoretical problem posed by this very simple postulate was, however, extremely perplexing. It meant that the comprehension of history had to take into account the uncertainty and contingency of human creativity. History had to be disclosed not as an inexorable march in one direction or another, not as a predestined fate carried out by unknowing puppets, not as a set of events which were completely explainable given their circumstances. Instead history had to be conceived as penetrated at all moments by the future, as always open to human intervention, as continuously full of surprises and unexpected possibilities. 'Everything changes if one considers that society is presented to each man as a *perspective of the future* and that this future penetrates to the heart of each one as a real motivation for his behaviour.'[7] The historical field that marxist theory proposed had to be one that brought into relief human actors making choices without total foreknowledge, projecting meanings without absolute justification, and finally creating a social world without final certainty of its validity or outcome. Marxism, in short, was a theory of human self-emancipation. A cardinal requirement of such a theory was that it make intelligible and proceed from the possibility that such emancipation could occur. We must, Sartre contended, 'rediscover in man his veritable humanity – that is, the power to make History by pursuing his own ends . . .'.[8]

It must be pointed out that there are no epistemological grounds upon which to sanctify absolutely the theoretical decision to conceptualise history from the perspective of revolution or creativity. One could argue with equal force that history is the action of God in the world or that it is an objective field of determined events. One must recognise, however, that in these cases, especially the latter, the theory will prove the assumption, the beginning will return to the end. History will be made intelligible in such a way that revolution is impossible and traces of human creativity will be ruled out from the beginning. Sartre argues correctly that alternative perspectives to that of Marx's dictum 'man makes history' must contain conservative political implications. Positivism, objectivism, determinism are possible theories of history but none of them are 'scientific' or value free. They all contain political implications that are anti-revolutionary.

Sartre carries the argument one step further. The episte-mological force of the marxist postulate that 'man makes history' is in the final analysis stronger than all others because, Sartre contends, it renders history intelligible at a more concrete level than the rest. The basis for this argument derives from a concept of human action (praxis) which combines marxist and existentialist elements. Sartre maintains that the historical field is composed of human actions and material things, subjects and objects. The human actions consist in projects or praxes which are defined as follows: human beings are set in specific situations (objectivity), which they interpret in given ways and act within and upon (subjectivity), which in turn places them in new specific situations (objectivity). They act by making projects. These consist in taking within perceptions of the situation, choosing to interpret those perceptions according to sets of criteria or values, and then acting, bringing out into the world, those choices.

> *Praxis*, indeed, is a passage from objective to objective through internalisation. The project, as the subjective surpassing of objectivity toward objectivity, and stretched between the objective conditions of the environment and the objective structures of the field of possibles, represents *in itself* the moving unity of subjectivity and objectivity, those cardinal determinants of activity. The subjective appears then as a necessary moment in the objective process.[9]

From the point of view of human action, history is a double movement of 'the internalisation of the external and the externalisation of the internal'.[10] As far as Sartre is concerned, marxism must recapture this process if it is to render history intelligible. Historical reason must retrace the projects of the past and only by doing so can it present history as the arena of human choices.

The project, for Sartre, has another quality which must be taken into account by historical materialism. That quality is totalisation. Each individual makes sense of the world in which he acts. Each project, however trivial, is an interpretation of the world and a valorisation of the world. To go to work in the ordinary way each day contains a choice, implicit or explicit, that the existing order of production, and the political and social systems that support it, cannot, at that moment, be overturned. A given project is connected with the larger project of living in the world at a determined time. <u>One can pretend not to take account of the totality, but that would be self-deception. Praxis necessarily totalises.</u> The historical field therefore includes as a main determinant not just the objective totality (the given state of the mode of production) but also the multiplicity of totalisations, the countless and intricately interlocked meanings given to the world by praxis. For Sartre history consists of changing totalisations embodied in praxis, encompassing moments of subjectivity and objectivity.

<u>The concepts of praxis, project and totalisation are intended by Sartre to restore to marxism its ability to capture the historical field from the point of view of revolution.</u> Such a reconstituted marxism would once again become the theoretical arm of the class struggle and it would also render marxism pre-eminent among all theories of history. There is a choice, as Sartre is wont to say, and this choice must be made. It consists in the following:

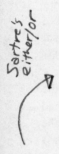

Sartre's either/or

> Only the project, as a mediation between two moments of objectivity, can account for history; that is, for human *creativity*. It is necessary to choose. In effect: either we reduce everything to identity (which amounts to substituting a mechanistic materialism for dialectical materialism) – or we make of dialectic a celestial law which imposes itself on the Universe, a metaphysical force which by itself engenders the historical process (and this is to fall back into Hegelian idealism) – <u>or we restore to the individual man his power to go beyond his situation by means of work and action.</u> This solution alone enables us to base the movement of totalisation *upon the real*.[11]

The entire claim of Sartre's marxism rests on the validity of this passage.

Surveying the theoretical landscape in 1960, Sartre discovered that marxists avoided the choice of revolution. In the East, marxist theory was an official doctrine of the state, justifying the politics of an established regime. In the West the opposite condition prevailed: the failure of the proletariat to win power was a practical and theoretical embarrassment to marxists. Social critics like Herbert Marcuse were willing to acknowledge the possibility that the working class no longer presented, in Western Europe and the United States, a negation to capitalist society.[12] Liberals rejoiced in the docility of the proletariat, announcing the integration of the working class into a pluralist world. The rising standard of living of factory workers contradicted the marxist thesis of progressive immiseration. Far from collapsing or being torn asunder, capitalism was able, in Marcuse's words, 'to deliver the goods'.

Faced with the political apathy of the working class, marxists salvaged the theory of class struggle by either limiting their discussions to the decolonisation movements of the Third World or continuing to denounce the evils of capitalism in the name of the militant, unified, revolutionary proletariat. Unwilling to face the theoretical consequences of the fact that the emperor wore no clothes, marxists stood by cheering the monarch of revolution without so much as a blush. For to confront the contemporary situation squarely would necessitate an account of the working class for which the traditional categories of historical materialism were inadequate. Instead the writings of marxists sounded more and more empty, the application of the formulas of historical materialism appeared more and more rigid and the heuristic value of socialist thought looked less and less compelling.

In such a context the French existential marxist sounded the tocsin of the revolutionary choice. Once the theoretical decision had been made to conceptualise the social-historical field from the vantage point of revolution, the question of the lack of class consciousness of the proletariat could no longer be evaded. To recapture its theoretical legitimacy marxism, in Sartre's hands, would go back and forth from the social totality to the individual and from the individual to society in search of the mediations that would account for the present circumstances. The progressive-regressive method was Sartre's name for the procedure through which concrete, living experience would become available to marxist thought. Rather than the repetitive intonation of categorical formulas, marxism would now enter the stream of history and render intelligible the particular condition of the working class. *A priori* notions deriving from traditions of radical thought would all be abandoned. Sartre's marxism began with the social structure and traced its markings in the individual. It then returned to the individual and followed his actions upon the social structure. 'The movement of comprehension', Sartre insisted, 'is simultaneously progressive (towards the objective result) and regressive (I go back towards the original condition).'[13] The new method opened marxism to the concrete, enabling it to examine how specific workers are affected by specific conditions of capitalism and how they respond to it, producing themselves, as Marx said, in the process of producing their world. One would then be able to comprehend precisely how revolution, the ever-present possibility of negating the system and acting to destroy it, existed in the social field and at the same time was denied and avoided in the routine of daily survival.

In the framework of individuals who internalised their situations and projected meanings back at the society, mediations were crucial to the process of comprehension. 'Marxism', Sartre warned, 'lacks any hierarchy of mediations which would permit it to grasp the process which produces the person and his product inside class and within a given society at a given historical moment.'[14] Burdened by a reflection theory of knowledge, in which ideas are the direct consequence of social structures, the dominant marxism of 1960 could not account for the absence of class consciousness, the ability of the capitalist system to interrupt the process of radicalisation. Although it was in the interests of the workers to oppose an exploitative society, they did not see it that way.

The reasons for this to Sartre were all too obvious. Workers experienced numerous social contexts, not only the factory. They participated in residential groups, families, communities, nations, in addition to workplaces. In each of these situations individuals faced choices and made commitments which in turn shaped their overall projects or totalisations. Between the individual and his or her work came the numerous mediations which could easily upset the applecart of class consciousness.

While marxism theorised society from the point of production, workers lived their lives everywhere. Sartre named especially the family as a mediation between the individual and society.

> Today's marxists are concerned only with adults; reading them, one would believe that we are born at the age when we earn our first wages. They have forgotten their own childhoods. As we read them, everything seems to happen as if men experienced their alienation and their reification *first in their own work*, whereas in actuality each one lives it *first*, as a child, *in his parents' work*.[15]

The basic projects of the individual are formed before he ever set foot in a workplace. Ethnic traditions, family myths, sibling relations, neighbourhood communities – all these experiences need to be taken into account. When marxism looks at the family it sees only an extension of the mode of production: the family is a unit of consumption, it is the place of the reproduction of labour power, it institutes a sexual division of labour, and so forth. While true, these perceptions do not allow for the *disjuncture* between the family and the mode of production. They allow only the further reinforcement of the workplace on the home. A renewed marxism, one that would account properly for mediations,

> discovers the point of insertion for man and his class – that is, the particular family – as a mediation between the universal class and the individual. The family in fact is constituted by and in the general movement of History, but is experienced, on the other hand, as an absolute in the depth and opaqueness of childhood.[16]

Sartre's insistence on the role of mediations was not a lapse into pluralism, or worse, empiricism. The introduction of levels of analysis outside the mode of production did not disturb the synthetic, totalising tendency which is a hallmark of marxism. The study of man outside his labour did not disrupt the general position of radical theory as a critique of political economy. Instead Sartre aimed at enriching marxism by enabling it to comprehend those numerous instances in which a class did not follow its class interests. He gave as an example the defence of economic liberalism by the girondins during the course of the French Revolution of 1789. Representing commerce and banking, this group defended *laissez-faire* economics in line with their class ideology even when a rational pursuit of economic interests would compel it to favour state interference in the economy. Marxist historians of the revolution had difficulty, however, explaining why the girondins failed to support economic controls instituted by the state as a means of defending the revolution against outside enemies. Holding passionately to their principle of economic freedom, the girondins came into conflict with the more 'rational' jacobins. But why keep to outmoded ideas? Such 'idealism' fell beyond the purview of historical materialism. To the marxists, Sartre proposed that when class interests contradict behaviour, the analysis need not terminate.

Pluralists, empiricists and positivists had no advantage over marxism. Their contributions were at best partial. Their analytic mode of thought, which chopped the social field into discrete pieces, might be used by marxists when it contributed to the comprehension of a particular mediation. But it was no substitute for marxism. The comprehension of society required, for Sartre, a totalising perspective, and here marxism, properly revised, was the surest key. Since the social world was in a process of transformation – one that included prominently the possibility of the overthrow of capitalism – only marxism was an adequate conceptual tool. In addition to fragmenting history to the point of unintelligibility, analytic methods tended to fall into objectivism. When, for example, American sociologists studied crime they concluded that criminals had certain traits. These traits inhered in the criminal like hardness in a stone. The attributes of the criminal were thing-like essences for the sociologist. In this way, analytical thought lost its capacity to illuminate living individuals who made certain choices in a given context and rejected others. For Sartre analytical reason necessarily fell into a false objectivism which slipped easily into ideology. American sociology contributed to legitimising capitalism by isolating the criminal from the conflictual totality and locating variables within him in a manner that precluded critical thought on the part of the scientist.

The practitioners of analytical reason were not alone, Sartre contended, in objectifying falsely the social field. Marxists too fell into positivism, in their case by removing from history its openness, its contingency, its multiplicity of meanings. A decade earlier, Merleau-Ponty criticized the marxist tendency towards determinism by arguing for a philosophy of history which brought into relief the contingency of human affairs.[17] Now Sartre, in his attempt to purge marxism of its epistemological errors, developed a similar argument.

In the nineteenth century, Marx laboured to give history a single meaning by theorising a future in which a unified proletariat would realise the ultimate stage of the class struggle. A telos of history would be unveiled through the creative action of the working class. Sartre wrote, 'History was finally to have a meaning for man. By becoming conscious of itself, the Proletariat becomes the subject of History; that is, it must recognise itself in History.'[18] During the course of the twentieth century, marxist writers increasingly defined the telos of history more and more narrowly, eliminating its character as a possible future for man in favour of that of a predetermined outcome. Dialectical necessity became little more than the mechanical necessity of an iron law of nature. In the computer of contemporary marxists, human history was programmed with the precision of a natural law.

For his part, Sartre would not deny the possibility of a single meaning to history, but he insisted that it be based on the future and that it not preclude polyvalence of meaning. There was no epistemological ground from which one could posit a single meaning of history. To collapse the events of the past into the homogeneous unfolding of some dialectical plan was to centre oneself as the metaphysical reference point of mankind. The result of such a theological strategy was to deny to history its necessary temporality, to reduce the times of the past to the privileged time of the theorist. The contingent choices of human beings in bygone ages would be appropriated improperly by the modern philosopher.

If history had no single meaning, Sartre would not deny that it could have one. If the theorist had no right to expropriate the multiplicity of choices from the past, he could legitimately – indeed, he must of necessity – develop a project for the future which would promise the chance for a teleological end. Sartre expressed the argument as follows:

> The plurality of *the meanings* of history can be discovered and posited for itself only upon the ground of a future totalisation – in terms of the future totalisation and in contradiction with it. It is our theoretical and practical duty to bring this totalisation closer every day. All is still obscure, and yet everything is in full light. To tackle the theoretical aspect, we have the instruments; we can establish the method. Our historical task, at the heart of this polyvalent world, is to bring closer the moment when History will have *only one meaning*, when it will tend to be dissolved in the concrete men who will make it in common.[19]

In this important passage Sartre made an argument that is likely to sound dissonant to both marxist and liberal ears.

In agreement with marxism, Sartre proclaimed that history could have one meaning; that epistemologically one could not write history without projecting on to it a single meaning; that if, in writing history (or thinking about society), one failed to do so, one incorrectly severed the tie between thought and practice. Granted Sartre's assumption that one theorises from the vantage point of a possible revolution (since only this assumption was compatible with the truth that man makes history), then it became incumbent upon the historian to project a telos on human affairs. The writing of history from a teleological perspective has, of course, been criticised relentlessly in recent years. The basic argument against it has been that it introduces determinism: that teleological history strips man of his freedom and imputes a false omniscience to the historian.

To a great extent, Sartre's position overcomes these objections because it also agrees with the liberal position in which history contains a multiplicity of meanings. In fact, for Sartre the one goes necessarily with the other. The concept of a single end to human

29

affairs can be made only if the historical theory posits the multiplicity of meanings to the past. According to Sartre, the historians must at one and the same time posit a future totalisation and reveal the plurality of meanings in the past. Only by recapturing the contingency of past actions in all their particularity can the historian connect them properly with the totalisation that he must project on the future. The liberal position, relying on analytical reason and retreating from the deterministic consequences of marxist teleology, incorrectly fragments the past into a false plurality and severs the vital umbilical cord linking the past with the present and the future. The marxist position, on the contrary, obsessed with the role of the proletariat in the class struggle and sceptical of the liberal's flight from the future, absorbs everything into teleology and fails to acknowledge the contingency that pervades the historical field.

The goal Sartre set for himself in the *Critique of Dialectical Reason* was nothing less than a synthesis of these positions, one that would resolve the epistemological riddle of history, grounding it in revolution and at the same time accounting for the reverses, breaks, fissures and discontinuities of the past. Sartre sought to save the marxist vision of man's future by rewriting the past in existentialist hues, by recapturing freedom in history. The concepts of praxis, project, totalisation, mediation, and the progressive-regressive method were all intended to shatter the illusionary dogmas of stalinist marxism, to open the past as the concrete place of human choice and creativity, to allow the dialectic to wend its way inconclusively, regressively, indirectly, not just progressively, in Sartre's own words 'to reconquer man within marxism'.

Search For a Method, written for a special issue of a Polish journal devoted to French intellectual currents, serves as a polemical prolegomenon to the main body of the *Critique of Dialectical Reason*. It raised the chief questions about the epistemological value of the marxist theory of history at a time when the march of events appeared as disconfirming evidence. In 1960 marxist writing suffered from economism and reductionism, the Soviet Union had drifted away from the vision of communist society, revolution was centred not in places with the most developed working classes, but in the periphery of decolonising peasant and tribal societies (like Algeria), blurred by and confused with struggles for national liberation. In this situation marxism was losing its credentials as a heuristic theory, becoming an ideological arm of Soviet foreign policy. In the short run marxism might live on the charisma of third world revolution. In the long run it would have to make intelligible an increasingly obscure direction of history. Sartre's *Critique* was written to reconstitute marxist theory at a time when the surface of events appeared to belie its epistemological value. The happy marriage between dialectical reason and revolution was on the rocks so Sartre offered himself as a much-needed counsellor.

2. The Limits of Dialectical Reason

The main body of the *Critique of Dialectical Reason*[1] is notorious for its impenetrability. It is written in a style that makes no concessions to the reader. Dense, involuted, repetitive, filled with difficult terminology and long digressions, it challenges the reader's fortitude. For example, Sartre invents new concepts for each shade of meaning. To designate social phenomena in which the dialectical quality of the project is absent, Sartre uses the following terms: processed matter, practico-inert, anti-dialectic, counter-finality, physis, exis and so on. If the *Critique* is uncompromising with the reader, it is equally relentless in pursuing a systematic interrogation of the dialectic. For that reason, the rewards for studying it are considerable.

The *Critique* opens with a long discussion of the problem of dialectical reason. According to Sartre, the advances made by Marx in developing historical materialism were not matched in epistemology. When Marx transformed Hegel's idealist dialectic, in which Absolute Spirit came to know itself through the unfolding of consciousness in history, into a materialist dialectic of the development of modes of production, he did not elaborate systematically the grounds for this new kind of knowledge. In Sartre's words, 'The totalising thought of historical materialism has established everything except its own existence.'[2] The absence of epistemological clarity in Marx's texts is responsible, Sartre admonished, for the continual lapse by marxists into positivism. Sartre argues that,

> Marx's originality lies in the fact that, in opposition to Hegel, he demonstrated that History *is in development*, that *Being is*

irreducible to Knowledge, and, also that he preserved the dialectical movement *both in* Being *and in* Knowledge. He was correct, *practically*. But having failed *to re-think the dialectic*, Marxists have played the positivist game.[3]

Sartre's serious charge against Marx was that he failed to establish the nature of dialectical truth. As a consequence, Marx and his followers took positions that were in fundamental contradiction to dialectical reason.

For Sartre, marxism was 'an unveiling of being, and at the same time . . . an unanswered question as to the validity of this unveiling'.[4] Marxism established the priority of being over knowledge without specifying the nature of this knowledge. As distinct from analytical reason, dialectical reason grasped the totality and conceptualised it as a process of self-transformation. Such a view implied a new relation between being and knowledge which transcended traditional materialism and idealism. The older views gave priority either to being or to knowledge, in both cases, however, conceiving the object as fixed. Marxist materialism gave priority to being but conceived it as changing. The dialectic was the changing nature of being; but, at the same time, it was the method or type of theory which made this transformation intelligible. Hence both being and knowledge were 'dialectical'. In Sartre's words,

> The dialectic is both a method *and* a movement in the object. For the dialectician, it is grounded on a fundamental claim both about the structure of the real and about that of our *praxis*. We assert simultaneously that the process of knowledge is dialectical, that the movement of the object . . . is *itself* dialectical, and that these two dialectics are one and the same.[5]

The claim that being and knowledge were identical seems to contradict the marxist postulate that being is prior to knowledge. This contradiction was only apparent. Sartre sought to transcend it by reminding the reader that the knower is not outside being, as in scientific and analytical reason, but within it. 'The dialectician . . . locates himself within a system.'[6] Dialectical reason is part of the dialectic of being and therein lies its true difficulties. It is possible to argue that being is both prior to and identical with knowledge as long as knowledge is understood to reside within being. In this case, knowledge simply traces the transformation of being. But, Sartre laments, this has not happened: marxists have not successfully captured the dialectic of history. Since marxist knowledge is in question, it is necessary to carry out a critique of it. But a critique requires a separation of the knower from the object; it implies a distance between the two.

The problem with such a critique, however, is that it steps outside its object and therefore is not dialectical. Dialectical reason remains within its object as part of it; the traditional (Kantian) notion of critique demands the separation of the knower and the known. Thus it appears that a critique of dialectical reason is a contradiction in terms. Commentators on Sartre's critique, like Raymond Aron, have not failed to point out this dilemma. Either one remains a marxist and epistemological clarity is impossible; or one is a Kantian and gives up dialectical reason in favour of certain knowledge.[7] In Aron's view, Sartre retreated from marxism and aligned himself with Kant.

But according to Sartre, a critique in the manner of Kant's famous *Critique of Pure Reason* was inadequate to the problematic of the dialectic since it was founded on an absolute separation of knowledge and being. Since, for dialecticians, knowledge was within being and the two were inseparable, the Kantian task of defining the categories of knowledge necessary to capture being was inadequate. Sartre insisted that were we 'to ground our dialectical categories on the impossibility of experience without them, as Kant did for positivist Reason, then we would indeed attain necessity, but we would have contaminated it with the opacity of fact'.[8] Thus the dilemma of a critique of dialectical reason could not be resolved by a resort to the strategy of Kant.

Nevertheless, a critique of dialectical reason, Sartre continued, must establish the epistemological value of that reason *a priori*. One could not discover the limits of dialectical reason by investigating specific studies that employed it. Dialectical reason cannot be discounted because of empirical failure, for to do so would still not demonstrate its epistemological value or lack of value. The method needed to be justified conceptually, not empirically, since any given use of the dialectic could be dismissed as faulty without discovering whether the method itself was of value.

In the marxist tradition, the effort to supply epistemological grounds for dialectical reason led most often to a reliance on a dialectic of nature. Sartre pointed to Engels who, in *Dialectics of Nature*, sought a transcendent legitimacy for dialectics by arguing that nature itself had the characteristics of the dialectic. Therefore dialectic was the law of the universe and hence could not be challenged. Sartre rejected this strategy for verifying the legitimacy of the dialectic. He granted that nature might be dialectical, although he insisted that we have no such knowledge at present. But he denied the project of a dialectic of nature since it implied that the certainty of dialectical knowledge was to be demonstrated through a procedure in which knowledge was autonomous and outside being. Because the scientific method required, as did all forms of analytical reason, a de-situated knower who was ontologically distanced from the object, one would not thereby prove the validity of dialectical reason which insisted on the implication of the knower in being. To validate dialectical reason on the basis of a dialectics of nature was to make it dependent upon a form of positivism, which was clearly impossible.

The critique of Engels clarified for Sartre some necessary features of his task: it led him to the position that the critique of dialectical reason must be sought within human history. Sartre wrote:

> The dialectic will be an effective method as long as it remains *necessary* as the law of intelligibility and as the rational structure of Being. A materialist dialectic will be meaningless if it cannot establish, within human history, the primacy of material conditions as they are discovered by the *praxis* of particular men and as they impose themselves on it. In short, if there is to be any such thing as dialectical materialism, it must be a *historical* materialism, that is to

35

say, a materialism from within; it must be one and the same thing to produce it and to have it imposed on one, to live it and to know it. Consequently, this materialism, if it exists, can be *true* only within the limits of our social universe.[9]

Dialectical reason found its object in social experience because, as Vico pointed out long ago, only this type of object is produced or created by the same type of being who is attempting to derive knowledge of it. In order for the knower to be within the known, the known must be like the knower. While it was true, Sartre granted, that man is within nature, man is not within nature in the same way as he is within society for the simple reason that man did not create nature, although he did make history.

By specifying the object of dialectical reason as history (or social being), Sartre moved one step closer to an adequate justification for a critique of dialectical reason. The question remains the following: How can one raise the the question of a 'critique' of dialectical reason when critique implies a de-situated knower and dialectic insists upon setting the knower within being. Sartre's response to this dilemma was precise and most important: history (or being) *itself* raises the question of a critique of dialectical reason; the dialectic foists upon the knower the problem of a critique. Therefore to carry out the project of a critique of dialectical reason does not de-situate the knower; on the contrary, the knower is responding to the very moment of dialectic. Sartre argues,

> Our problem is *critical*. Doubtless this problem is itself raised by History. But it is precisely a matter of testing, criticising and establishing, *within History* and at this particular moment in the development of human societies, the instruments of thought by means of which History thinks itself in so far as they are also the practical instrumentalities by means of which it is made.[10]

Dialectical reason is subject to a critique precisely because it is in crisis at this moment in time. Sartre's explanation for the crisis contains no surprises. Marxist theory has become reduced to mechanical formulas by its connection with the soviet state.

Therefore it no longer acts as an instrument of intelligibility: 'critical investigation could not occur *in our history,* before stalinist idealism had sclerosed both epistemological methods and practices'.[11]

Sartre's effort to situate the critical moment within history is subject to the criticism that Sartre's knowledge of this crisis of dialectical thought is itself unproven by dialectical reason. In other words, the objection might be raised that Sartre is relying upon a totalisation (that stalinism has corrupted marxism) which itself requires dialectical reason for proof. But since dialectical reason has not been determined as a legitimate form of knowing, one cannot base one's critique on an empirical instance of it. The charge in short is that Sartre's argument is circular.

Circularity, however, is a characteristic of all knowledge, Sartre countered. In fact, in this instance, circularity is required. Sartre began, let us recall, with the project of revolution. From this point it is entirely legitimate to totalise the social field and discover the problem of marxism's weakness. Indeed, Sartre claims that knowledge (dialectical knowledge) is impossible today because of the inadequacies of stalinist marxism. Sartre was led to the project of a critique from the impossibility of knowing the social field as part of the process of changing it. The fact that Sartre employed a judgment based on dialectical reason (that stalinism led to a crisis of marxism) as the basis for a critique of dialectical reason is not a contradiction but a necessary circularity. After demonstrating the possibility of a critique of dialectical reason, Sartre went on to outline the nature of his task. What precisely is dialectical reason and how can one provide a critique of it?

Sartre defines dialectical reason as the 'movement of totalisation' and as a 'moment of the totalisation'. The dialectic is the movement of history in which the totality is seen as a temporal, synthetic unification. Totality as distinct from totalisation is a whole dominated by spatiality rather than temporality. Like a painting or a machine, a totality derives its unity from a *past* action, not from the present or the future. It is, in Sartre's words, fundamentally inert and passive. Society is often conceptualised as a totality, for instance by structural-functionalists. Here society appears as an integrated conglomeration of fixed attributes, each of which is characterised in spatial terms. Such a view of society is undialectical because it cannot account for negation.

In the opposite manner, a dialectical perspective sees society as a totalisation, as a process of unification which is pervaded by temporality and negation. The unity of a totalisation captures a continuous process of negation: nothing is fixed; everything is being determined, cancelled and determined anew. The task of dialectical reason is simply to make intelligible the totalisation. Dialectical reason is, Sartre claims, 'the very movement of totalisation'.

This definition of dialectical reason appears to reduce knowledge to a reflection of reality. Such is not the case, however, because reason must itself become a 'moment of the totalisation', must itself be totalising. While Sartre writes that the only laws of the dialectic are 'the rules produced by the developing totalisation',[12] he also posits an active role for dialectical reason. Arguing against both the Kantian position of the scientific, external observer and the Leninist position of the internal, determined thinker, Sartre characterises dialectical reason as both internal to the totalisation and as a determinant of it:

> Critical investigation takes place *inside* the totalisation and can be neither a contemplative recognition of the totalising movement, nor a particular autonomous totalisation of the known totalisation. Rather, it is a real moment of the developing totalisation in so far as this is embodied in all its parts and is realised as synthetic knowledge of itself through the mediation of certain of these parts.[13]

The knower is both within and apart from the known; he traces the movement of the real and changes the real in doing so; he reflects objective reality and generates categories by acts of reason to make that reality intelligible.

It is worth pointing out that Louis Althusser, who regarded Sartre's *Critique* as an unfortunate example of humanism and has been consistently opposed to Sartre, presented the identical position against Marx's inadequate epistemology.[14] Althusser presented his own theoretical advance a few years after the appearance of the *Critique*, announcing that Marx's 'immense theoretical revolution' was lacking an epistemological justification. In his hands, however, the task of developing the foundations of marxist knowledge led not to Sartre's existential marxism but to a structuralist marxism that claimed for itself scientific status and resembled traditional positivism all too closely.

The inadequacy of Althusser's criticism of Sartre is apparent. Claiming that Sartre was a mere empiricist who traced the movement of the dialectic, Althusser favoured a theoretical practice which produced concepts, such as the mode of production. For Althusser knowledge was the autonomous creation by the scientist of the categories that illuminated empirical reality. Yet Sartre also provided such a 'theoretical practice'. He viewed his task as that of establishing *'a priori* ... the heuristic value of the dialectical method'.[15] Far from empiricism, Sartre's method imposed on theory the job of generating categories, prior to any historical investigation, which provided the tools for the reconstruction of totalisation. Unlike Althusser, however, Sartre refused the stance of the pure external observer and theorist. Sartre overcame Althusser's Kantianism by placing the process of theoretical production within the developing totalisation, thereby preserving the link of knower and known, theory and practice.

Certain additional accusations made by Althusser against Sartre deserve comment and refutation. Althusser, associating himself with structuralism, criticised the alleged humanism of Sartre's position. In line with the polemic of Michel Foucault and others that 'man is dead', Althusser strove for a 'theoretical anti-humanism' which placed marxism beyond ethical moralism. Humanism was false, for Althusser, because it discounted the scientific claims of marxism. Yet in 1960, before Foucault and before Althusser, Sartre, wrote in refutation of liberalism 'it must be understood that there is no such thing as man'.[16] In this way, Sartre's *Critique* cannot be dismissed as a humanist tract that makes of marxism yet another arbitrary ethical dogma.

Additional evidence that Sartre is not an empiricist is found in his critique of the position of Wilhelm Dilthey. This late-nineteenth century German philosopher of history wanted to distinguish historical knowledge from the natural sciences. In this way he would achieve, following the Kantian formula, a critique of historical knowledge, the same task as Sartre set for himself. Dilthey developed a theory of comprehension (*verstehen*) in which the historian recaptures the past not by standing outside it and observing it 'objectively', but by an interior, sympathetic grasp of the historical figure. The historian could place himself in the shoes of the historical figure and imaginatively recreate his ideas, motives and values.

Sartre, on the contrary, distinguishes clearly between comprehension and what he terms 'intellection'. Somewhat like Dilthey, Sartre defines comprehension as the grasp of intentionality. He writes, 'Whenever a *praxis* can be traced to the intention of a practical organism or of a group, even if this intention is implicit or obscure to the agent himself, there is comprehension.'[17] With the totalisation, there are times when a group pursues ends that are displayed in their praxis. At such times, human action attains transparency to the actors and to observers. An act of empathy or identification by the historian can bring back this historical moment and make it intelligible. Most of history, for Sartre, does not display these traits. Instead, under normal circumstances, praxis cannot be traced back directly to the agency of a group. In the vast majority of cases, human history is composed of meanings that are lost to human subjects, meanings that have long before been alienated from them. These dead meanings require a different logic from that of comprehension. Sartre's term for the operations required by the historian to place these meanings in the totalisation is intellection. This form of knowledge is far more complex than comprehension and it is inacessible to the Diltheyan quest for intentions.

The goal of providing a critique of dialectical reason engages Sartre in precisely-defined tasks. He does not here attempt to write history, to trace the totalisation, to map the contours of the dialectic: 'our task', he writes, 'cannot *in any way* be to reconstruct real History in its development, any more than it can consist in a concrete study of forms of production or of the groups studied by the sociologist and the ethnographer'.[18] Instead, Sartre's aim in the *Critique* is to test the intelligibility of dialectical reason by generating categories that are congruent with it and to investigate whether these categories are adequate to the forms of human action. Put differently, since marxism in its current forms, does not make intelligible the varieties of human action, the validity of dialectical thought is in doubt. If marxism is to be preserved as a form of knowledge, new 'instruments of thought', as Sartre says, must be developed that can portray the social field convincingly.

Behind Sartre's far-reaching condemnation of Soviet-dominated marxist theory lay a set of problems that has always beset historical materialism, but which Sartre does not adequately specify. Granted the epistemological deficiencies of marxism and granted its tendency to objectify the social field—charges which Sartre makes explicitly—what lurks within the *Critique* in addition to these, and is perhaps in the last analysis more important than them, is that marxism cannot adequately account for class consciousness or subjectivity. For Marx, individuals in a class could become aware of the way their class position (their relation to the means of production) limited and oppressed them. If they did and if they acted on that awareness politically, they were class conscious. If not, they had false consciousness. Marx presumed that attaining class consciousness did not require herculean philosophical labours. It was easier for the proletariat to attain class consciousness than the peasantry because workers were brought together in the misery of their everyday life. Collective praxis in the factory encouraged, Marx thought, group recognition of oppression and the need to act collectively against it. A model of rational self-interest haunts the marxist notion of consciousness. Peasants might lapse into false consciousness because of their isolated mode of production, but such was not the case for workers who could not avoid the direct insight that their life could be improved only by overthrowing the system of capitalism.

Marx was aware of the innumerable obstacles that might

intercede between the worker and his class consciousness. He described in detail many cases where ethnic and religious differences, national loyalties, factors of race and so forth could divide and separate workers, causing them to squabble among themselves instead of uniting for the revolution. He was also prescient about the role of the ruling class in dissembling, prevaricating, and machinating endlessly to obscure from the workers the true causes of their misery. Politicians engaged in foreign wars and imperial adventures in order to shift the focus of attention from civil strife to distant threats. Capitalists vituperated against union organisers and militants, charging them with crimes and accusing them of immorality, casting them in workers' eyes as foreign agents or alien beings. These for Marx were the operations of ideology, ruling class hegemony working to disrupt the solidarity of the proletariat. The workers, he thought, could overcome these powerful forces of false consciousness. But he did not develop categories of subjectivity that would trace the rise to class consciousness. One suspects that he preserved an unarticulated faith in the prominence of material conditions, and that, like the liberal humanists of the bourgeoisie, he was caught in a utilitarian logic of interest in material well-being.

In any case, the history of the past century argues compellingly that workers do not readily attain revolutionary class consciousness and that understanding the process through which they might do so requires the development of new categories of thought. It is after the world wars, the depression, and the experience of fascism, when class consciousness appeared least pressing, least prominent in the landscape of social action, that Sartre attempted to pose the question: how can the labyrinth of false consciousness during the past century be made intelligible and how can the possibility of class consciousness be reasserted? These questions inform the basic problematic of the *Critique of Dialectical Reason*. The importance of the problem of subjectivity is particularly clear in Sartre's concepts of reciprocity and the individual. At the base of all history, Sartre proposes, is 'the synthetic bond of reciprocity'.

> We are proposing not the rewriting of human history, but the critical investigation of bonds of interiority . . . or, in other words, the discovery, in connection with real, though quite ordinary, undertakings, structures and events, of the answer to this all-important question: in the process of human history, what is the respective role of relations of interiority and exteriority?[19]

If history is no more than a set of changing objective relations (modes of production, institutions, and so forth), then class consciousness is not a problem. If on the contrary one conceives of history in terms of bonds between people, specifically of bonds based on the possibility of mutual recognition, one can develop a view of history as a logic of freedom. Eschewing notions of human nature,[20] one can test the proposition that human beings can attain freedom through the recognition of freedom in the other and in the consequent action of solidary groups pursuing this freedom.

As a body of knowledge marxism has failed to illuminate class consciousness because, states Sartre, it has not explored the ways in which men live their freedom with others, at the subjective level, in the mode of alienation or oppression. Only a focus on the 'bonds of interiority' can illuminate the process in which class consciousness becomes false consciousness and in turn may re-emerge as class consciousness. Sartre thus presupposes that a particular form of bonds of interiority is possible, one in which the action and consciousness of each individual depends on the mutual recognition of freedom.

From the vantage point of the concept of 'bonds of reciprocity', history unfolds through the praxis of individuals. Sartre takes the individual's conscious action (or praxis) as the starting point, not because he is an existentialist and hence reduces social reality to the individual, but because the subjective processes of mutual recognition are played out through the meanings embodied in individuals. The dialectical history of totalisations, paradoxically, commences with the individual. Sartre writes that the critical investigation

Will set out from the immediate, that is to say from the individual fulfilling himself in his abstract *praxis*, so as to rediscover, through deeper and deeper conditionings, the totality of his practical bonds with others and, thereby, the structures of the various practical multiplicities and, through their contradictions and struggles, the absolute concrete: historical man.[21]

The test of dialectical reason begins with the individual as the phenomenon closest, or most 'immediate', to the investigator or the reader. Dialectical reason will have to prove its powers continuously by permitting the investigator/reader to discover him or herself in the historical process. The grand panorama of history must be connected with the minutiae of the individual's experience. Sartre writes, 'The locus of our critical investigation is none other than the fundamental identity between an individual life and human history.'[22]

The identity between the individual and history does not imply that the life of the individual recapitulates the life of the species. Sartre is not relying on the biological analogy. The bond between the individual and history is epistemological: the dialectical view of history must be able to render the experiences of individuals intelligible to them. It must be able to convince individuals that their life is part of history, that it can only be understood by relating it to history, and that only by taking a stance within history, by totalising their own experience, can the movement of emancipation become intelligible to them as a concrete possibility.

Sartre has been accused, falsely I believe, of privileging the individual in the manner of liberal social theory.[23] It has been argued that Sartre's emphasis on the individual prevents him from being a marxist. Sartre's individualism in the *Critique* is traced back to his earlier, pre-political phase in *Being and Nothingness* where isolated individuals were de-situated and ahistorical. Whatever the merits of this position regarding *Being and Nothingness*, it has little force when applied to the *Critique*. Here Sartre's concept of the individual does not serve as an opposite term to society or history. What Sartre is after is the connection between the two because, he believes, only in this way can one demonstrate the penetration of social forms in individual life and therefore the thorough implication of the individual in history. Unlike liberal social theory, Sartre's view of the individual does not seek to preserve an essential human nature from contamination by society. He does not, in the manner of Locke, hypothesise a pre-social individual who later joins society only to uphold better private property or freedom of choice. Sartre is not led to an atomistic view of society in which individual monads circulate without being touched deeply by their intercourse. Indeed, he states explicitly that *'there is no such thing* as an isolated individual'.[24] On the contrary, Sartre's individual is formed and transformed through social interactions, as we will see in chapter four below.

Nevertheless, there are times in Sartre's text where he speaks of the individual in a manner that is reminiscent of traditional liberal theory. In certain places Sartre's argument falls back from a marxist perspective, sounding much like a defence of individual autonomy against the corruption of social exchange. In these cases, Sartre lapses from his aim of dialectical totalisation towards a monadic view of the individual. The neo-marxism of the Frankfurt school has the same tendency. The texts of Horkheimer, Marcuse and Adorno often read like celebrations of individual autonomy against the undesirable dependency of social relations. It cannot be seriously maintained, however, that the main arguments of the *Critique* suffer from such tendencies.*

---

* A more serious objection against Sartre's concept of the totalising individual can be raised from the perspective of Jacques Derrida, who has effectively criticised efforts such as Sartre's to conceptualise the totality. To Derrida, Sartre's *Critique* participates in the 'logocentrism' of the Western philosophical tradition.[25] From this perspective, the notion of the totalising individual relies on a metaphysics of presence in which the truth captured by the totaliser serves as a transcendental signified. A 'deconstruction' of Sartre's *Critique* would show that the concept of totalisation falls into the same difficulty as Plato's notion of the idea and Hegel's Absolute Knowledge. In each case, Truth is centred in a philosophical subject who asserts the presence of the real in the idea. In Sartre's case, history becomes the totalisation as known by the individual. The gap or difference between the real and the known is broken in the mind of the totaliser who pretends to embody the truth.

This Derridean argument, while containing some validity, is subject to the following objection. Every strategy of knowing, every epistemological act, implies a claim of certainty of some sort. Knowledge, if it signifies anything, means the centering of truth in the knower, the drawing in of the true to the thinker. The problem which Derrida properly raises is that intellection is often privileged by the philosopher in such a way that the necessary distinction between the concept and the object is abolished. In Sartre's case this problem is minimised through the link established between theory and praxis. The reflexivity of Sartre's *Critique*, its self-conscious grounding in the situation of the theorist, prevents the absorption of the object in the idea. As long as dialectical reason is rooted in the historical context, the tendency to identify the real with the idea of the real is continuously undercut. In short, truth is present to the individual-totaliser only to the extent necessary to render history intelligible at this moment. Because temporality is built into dialectical intelligibility, no claim of absolute presence can be asserted.

The temporality and contextuality of the dialectician leads, in Derrida's eyes, to a second type of difficulty. Another form that logocentrism assumes in the Western philosophical tradition is that of teleology, as exemplified in Hegel and Marx. In this case, the philosophical text recaptures the past by concentrating all meaning in a telos or end. From the perspective of a future communist society, all of history is exhausted in the play of alienation and the end of alienation. In Hegel's version, history is recuperated completely and unified totally in Absolute Knowledge. The telos serves to homogenise the past, obliterating all differences in a firmly centred future.

The three moments of temporality – past, present and future – can each become the subject of this form of logocentrism. For the nineteenth-century German historian and philosopher of history, Otto von Ranke, the historian represents the past 'as it actually was', thereby collapsing the difference between the historian's present and history's past. While for the Italian idealist philosopher, Benedetto Croce, all history is contemporary history, thereby denying the separation of the historian from his object. For Hegel–Marx (and Sartre) the future-telos serves as the illusionary centre of the discourse. By deconstructing the aporias of temporality, Derrida threatens the prospects of Sartre's project.

The Derridean critique is instructive but not decisive. As a science of writing, Derrida's grammatology stresses the necessary difference between writing and speech, refusing the traditional philosophical priority given to speech. By inserting the form of writing between truth and speech, by denying that writing is a mere secondary representation of or supplement to speech, Derrida deflates the epistemological pretensions of logos. Thus Sartre's totalisation will always remain a concept in a text; it will not embody the truth of the age. Yet the totalisation must be a written inscription; it cannot be diminished because it is not something else,

Having examined the claims of Sartre's critics, we can now restate the limited purposes of his investigation. The *Critique of Dialectical Reason* will investigate the extent to which forms of human action can be made intelligible through concepts that are grounded in the view that 'man makes history'. Sartre is not seeking 'to discover the movement of History, the evolution of labour or of the relations of production, or class conflicts'.[27] Instead his 'goal is simply to reveal and establish dialectical rationality, that is to say, the complex play of *praxis* and totalisation'.[28] The *Critique* must be read with these limited purposes in mind. If not, the reader will mistake Sartre's concepts for historical facts and find them wanting.

Sartre characterises the *Critique* as the first volume of a larger study that will include, in a second volume, the progressive moment in which the movement of history is traced. This promise has not been fulfilled. After 1960 Sartre wrote three long volumes on Flaubert in which he applied the concepts of the *Critique* to an analysis of that nineteenth-century novelist. This is not the place to explain why Sartre was unable to complete volume two, but *Sartre's Marxism*, it is hoped, will contribute to that end by encouraging others to employ Sartre's concepts in their historical investigations.

The *Critique* is limited to the 'regressive' moment. It enumerates the categories through which history can be understood.

---

something outside it which claims ontological priority. Derrida upholds the textuality of writing, cautioning all philosophical tendencies to avoid the reduction of writing to a non-textual presence.

The text, as Sartre argues, is nevertheless inserted in a social field and derives from that field. To the extent that Derrida never goes beyond the text, he constructs by implication a reality consisting only of texts. (There are some phrases in *Of Grammatology* which characterise the present as the closure of the Western philosophical tradition and the opening of an age of writing. But this is done elliptically and without conviction, leaving Derrida's own text unclarified as to its political implications.)[26] For that reason he does not confront the problematic of Sartre's marxism which questions how theory can, in the present, make history intelligible from the point of view of revolution. Sartre is concerned with the play between text and world; Derrida insists that the text is neither a pale reflection of the world or a substitute for it.

Sartre anticipates that the categories generated in the *Critique* will unveil the nature of totalisation as 'the logic of freedom' in which the possibility will be demonstrated that there can be '*one* human history, with *one* truth and *one* intelligibility'.[29] The importance of the *Critique* derives from just this claim. Sartre is arguing that revolutionary theory can be consistent with the nature of revolution – historical materialism can conceptualise the proposition that man makes history. He is also maintaining that such a theory need not deny the contingency of history or the situatedness of the theorist. Dialectical reason cannot claim an authority for itself that rests outside the process of historical action. Dialectical reason, at once the intelligibility of history and part of history, cannot claim for itself a certainty that rests in transcendental reason, or in the party. If Sartre is correct, the gap between revolutionary theory and revolutionary movements, a gap that had produced such terrible effects in the past, may be closed.

3. 'Men and Things'

After the discussion of the goal and limits of the *Critique* Sartre gets down to the task of elaborating the categories necessary for a dialectical comprehension of any moment of history. These instruments of thought will enable Sartre to trace the movement of totalisation in the uncompleted second volume of the *Critique*. Sartre refers to the section of the *Critique* in which the categories are generated as the regressive moment, leaving the unfinished second volume of the *Critique* as the progressive moment. This is mis-leading, I think, because the progressive-regressive method, according to Sartre's definition, applies opposite strategies of comprehension to an historical subject. The subject of the *Critique*, volume one, however, is not historical. Here Sartre engages in theoretical work. He elaborates categories that may be applied within the domain of history, within the context of the project of scarcity. Only the second volume promises historical analysis properly so called. There Sartre will need to use both progressive and regressive methods, moving from the project to the social world and back from the social world to the project. This confusion, for which Sartre may be held liable, has contributed to serious misunder-standings of the *Critique* by several commentators.

Sartre outlines his categories in two broad sections. The first, to which we will turn in this chapter, is devoted to the relation between 'men and things' in which things present the greater force and meaning. The second, discussed in the following chapter, is devoted to those situations in which human beings have the determining force in establishing the intelligibility of the situation. In both cases, there is a mixture of human beings and things; only the emphasis is different. On a second level, however, these sections may be viewed as moving from the abstract to the concrete. They begin with a simple juxtaposition of an individual with nature and end with complex aggregates of relations between people and between people and things. In either case, it must be kept in mind that the underlying purpose of these sections is the theoretical elaboration of the categories of dialectical intelligibility.

Sartre begins with a reformulation of the relation between subject and object which is the central question of dialectical thought. Subject and object become for him 'men' and 'things' and their relation is one of mediation. 'The crucial discovery of dialectical investigation', Sartre writes, 'is that man is "mediated" by things to the same extent as things are "mediated" by man.'[1] For too long marxists had forgotten that historical materialism was founded in a dialectic of subject and object. Falling into a simplistic materialism, marxists have tended to posit the primacy of matter, reducing the social field to one of pure objects. The subjective side of the dialectic atrophied as it was relegated to the position of mere reflection. Sartre aimed at restoring the dialectic to its full power by equalising both sides of the issue, subject and object. His position is supported by reference to Marx in the 'Theses on Feuerbach'. There Marx criticised both idealism and materialism, the former for obscuring the object and the latter for omitting the active side of historical reality.[2] In the context of German idealism, Marx's historical materialism was meant to restore the force of objectivity to the practical world of human action. It was not meant to deny the active nature of subjectivity.

The danger in Sartre's restoration of the subject-object dialectic lay in a return to Hegelian idealism in which the object lost its power and the dialectic was reduced to pure subjectivity. Searching for an active subject, the theorist might eliminate objectivity altogether. This tendency had befallen Lukacs in *History and Class Consciousness*. The problematic of locating a class in and for itself led Lukacs to posit the proletariat as a pure agent of history. History itself became nothing other than the telos of an identical subject-object. Lukacs's mistake was his collapsing the tension in the dialectic in favour of subjectivity. Sartre's difficult task was to develop categories which would minimise the tendency in marxism to overlook one side of the dialectic.

The formula used by Sartre of human beings and things mediating each other would not satisfy everyone. Many critics accused him of returning not to Hegel's idealism but to Descartes' dualism. These commentators saw in the *Critique* an ontology of mind and matter, the cartesian *res cogitans* and *res extensa*. The panoply of categories minutely traced by Sartre rested, for them, on the decidedly un-marxist dualism of 'men and things'. These commentators claimed further that the entire edifice of the *Critique* was little more than a disguise for Sartre's ontology from *Being and Nothingness* in which the in-itself and the for-itself wrestled unendingly in a futile charade of existential disgust. Nothing could be less marxist for them than Sartre's crypto-existentialism, albeit dressed in the cloth of social theory.

Against these detractors it must be maintained that the dualism of human beings and things serves in the *Critique* as a support for the subject-object dialectic, not as a method of reintroducing the ontology of *Being and Nothingness*. Furthermore, the emphasis in the duality of human beings and things falls on their mediation, not on their opposition. Finally, these categories do not become sedimented into an ontology or a theory of being in the *Critique*. Instead, they serve as a point of departure for the elaboration of the main categories which themselves are the centre of dialectical reason for Sartre. If the cloth of the dialectic revealed only the pattern of human beings and things certainly Sartre's project would be a failure. If instead it brought into relief concepts necessary to render history intelligible as a subject-object dialectic, a different verdict would have to be rendered. Although, as we shall see, there are important deficiencies in the categories developed in the *Critique*, they do not pertain to an alleged residue of cartesianism.

Armed with the notions of project and totalisation, Sartre begins the elaboration of categories in which things take precedence over human beings with the concept of need. Individuals, faced with a natural environment, experience hunger. Their need becomes the occasion through which they totalise the field before them. At this moment, the field takes on a new meaning. It is no longer simply a world of natural objects. Instead it is divided into objects that can satisfy the need and those that cannot. Everything in the perceptual field has taken on a new significance. It has become reorganised in relation to the need of the individual. Its aesthetic qualities, its colours, its blend of movement and rest, become subordinated in the new totalisation. The field is reorganised in terms of how each element contributes to or detracts from the purpose of satisfying hunger. The rock over there becomes an impediment; the stream down below becomes a possible repository of fish. Of course, individual need is an abstract or over-simplified moment of the dialectic. It will serve not as a final category of analysis but as an illustration of the way an individual totalises the field as an opening into a more complex reality.

In order to satisfy their needs individuals must transform more than the social field. They must make themselves into tools. Their feet become locomotors; their arms levers; their brains calculators. In short, individuals have introduced into themselves features of the material world. They have given themselves passive qualities inhering in things in order to carry out their projects. Human beings are thus compelled to internalise the inertia of the natural world in the context of their totalisations. They become like things in the course of praxis. For Sartre this illustrates how profoundly things can mediate human beings. It also indicates that when human beings become like things it is because of their own action. Sartre says that 'it is through man that negation comes to man and to matter'.[3] The individual in need negated himself as an active subject, one free to constitute for himself the meanings of the social field, and transformed himself into a tool, a thing. The quality of negation, of redefining the significations of a situation, comes about through the praxis of human beings. It occurs to the extent that human beings can take on the quality of things.

An act of labour, as has been described, sets in motion a

profound transformation in the relations of human beings and things. In Sartre's words,

> The meaning of human labour is that man is reduced to inorganic materiality in order to act materially on matter and to change his material life. Through trans-substantiation, the project inscribed by our bodies in a thing takes on the substantial characteristics of the thing without altogether losing its original qualities.[4]

At the simplest level of dialectical intelligibility – an individual acting to satisfy a need – the most profound change in the relation of subject and object is enacted. In Marx, and later in Lukacs, the same transformation was recognised, but it was attributed to the capitalist system. For them, the capitalist mode of production generated the appearance that human beings were things and things were human. The fetish of the commodity produced the illusion of the reversal of subject and object. In Sartre's *Critique* this reversal is not limited to capitalism. Instead it serves analytically as the extreme case of the numerous possible ways in which human beings and things can interact. Furthermore, for Sartre the reversal is not merely an objective feature of a social system. Human beings do not become things only in appearance. They undergo, as we have seen, a profound interior alteration.

The example of the individual satisfying a need is a prologue to the comprehension of relations in which matter determines human beings. Since the project of the *Critique* is to test the intelligibility of dialectical reason and since dialectical reason applies only to history, the totalisation of the need remains too abstract. Rather than need, Sartre begins with scarcity. He posits scarcity as the great historical project which implicates everyone. Scarcity does not arise from an individual determining the social field through need, but from the entire society totalising the field as one of scarcity which is the basis of history: '. . . the relation of surrounding materiality to individuals is expressed *in our History* in a particular and contingent form since the whole of human development, at least up to now, has been a bitter struggle against *scarcity*'.[5] Sartre makes no effort to document the prevalence of scarcity, to prove that this individual or that intended to totalise the social field in this way. Nor does he attempt to date the origin of the project of scarcity, to locate its beginnings in ancient Greece or Rome. He simply takes it as a given.

Marxists have been quick to point out that Sartre's notion of scarcity conflicts seriously with basic tenets of historical materialism.[6] For Marx and Engels, modes of production always produce conflict since they create a *surplus*, not a scarcity, which is appropriated by a ruling class. The critical category at the centre of marxist thought is exploitation which maintains that the oppressed class labours not only to sustain itself but to produce value for a non-labouring class: a priesthood, a warrior aristocracy, or owners of capital. Far from viewing history as a realm of scarcity, marxism directs attention to the unjust distribution of surplus goods.

Critics of Sartre also point out that the concept of scarcity is a favourite piece in the ideology of liberalism. Capitalist political economy, not marxism, places scarcity at the centre of social theory and argues that the capitalist system resolves the problem of scarcity best by setting in motion the most efficient use of resources. Taking scarcity as a given, classical economic theory views the market as the best mechanism to distribute scarce goods. The dismal philosophy of capitalism requires the concept of scarcity to justify the inhumanity and impersonality of its institutions. The brutal competition of human against human, capital against capital, finds its legitimation only through the assumption of a scarce world of goods.

These arguments are not an effective refutation of Sartre's concept of scarcity. While it is true that Marx and Engels saw the extraction of surplus from the labouring class as the dynamic centre of a mode of production, they did not argue that this 'surplus' was enough to satisfy the needs of everyone in the society. Sartre's concept of scarcity does not negate the exploitative nature of class society. It is directed at a different level, one concerning the relation of the entire society to nature. Marx and Engels themselves recognised the need to conceptualise scarcity in Sartre's sense by referring to the long-term struggle between man and nature. For them the realm of freedom was separated from the realm of necessity by the inadequacy of human labour to satisfy human needs.[7] At one level the ruling class of each society extracts goods from the labouring class; at another level society as a whole, with all its economic resources, is unable to fulfil the needs of its members. If the elite few have been able to live in relative abundance, at no time has it been possible for everyone to enjoy wealth. Sartre's concept of scarcity points to the general fact that there has not been enough goods and it can be likened to Marx's notion of the realm of necessity in which brutalising labour is required to satisfy minimal needs.

The second argument raised against Sartre's concept of scarcity is also inconclusive. It is not true that Sartre joins the camp of the Hobbesians who see life as a miserable struggle over scanty crumbs. Unlike classical economic theorists, Sartre does not posit an external scarcity which requires the harsh, unyielding mechanisms of capitalism. Indeed he contends the opposite: 'scarcity is contingent', he writes. Scarcity is prevalent in human history only because human beings have decided to totalise the social field as one in which there is not enough. Far from a simple natural fact, scarcity is a human project. Far from being eternal, scarcity is relative. Sartre writes,

> For an historian situated in 1957, scarcity is not the basis of the possibility of *all* History. We have no way of telling whether, for different organisms on other planets — or for our descendants, if technical and social changes shatter the framework of scarcity — a different History, constituted on another basis, and with different motive forces and different internal projects, might be logically conceivable.[8]

More than that, Sartre points out that the argument in favour of natural scarcity is losing its verisimilitude with the advance of technology. The locus of scarcity in the advanced societies today is not the struggle against nature, but the struggle against forms of domination generated within the context of the struggle against nature. Far from a natural given, scarcity today is socially produced.

To some degreee Sartre justifies his choice of beginning with a concept of scarcity by reference to the continuing poverty in the third world. Advanced technology, whatever its successes, does not allow the critical theorist to overlook the widespread misery that persists. 'The fact is', Sartre reminds both liberals and marxists, 'that after thousands of years of History, three-quarters of the world's population are undernourished.'[9] Yet the main purpose for Sartre of emphasising scarcity comes not from the need to point out the obvious but from the need for a framework in which to locate at the broadest level the relations between human beings and things.

Scarcity is the primordial determination by matter of human relations. Human beings have given the meaning to the social field in which there is not enough for everyone. This determination comes back to haunt human relations. Scarcity is the negative horror, the violence that everyone performs over and over again against everyone else. People cannot recognise their mutual humanity, their basic freedom to create history together, because they are opposed to one another in a fundamental sense. Because of scarcity some will be designated as expendables. Some people will be designated as non-human in relation to scarce resources and every person will bear the mark of non-humanity since it is possible that they too can be so designated. Sartre explains,

> It must therefore be understood both that man's non-humanity does not come from his nature, and that far from excluding his humanity, it can only be understood through it. But it must also be understood that, as long as the reign of scarcity continues, *each and every man* will contain an inert structure of non-humanity which is in fact no more than material negation which has been interiorised.[10]

The project of scarcity, initiated by human beings and inaugurating the epoch of history, comes back into human relations, marking them with the sign of matter. Matter intrudes upon human relations at the subjective level, transforming reciprocity into violence, the human into the non-human.

Although the notion of scarcity undercuts the progressive optimism of the conquest of nature, it does not refute the possibility of communism, of a society beyond scarcity. Scarcity, for Sartre,

> is not a permanent structure, in the sense that it must always remain rigid and inert at a given level of human density, but rather a certain moment of human relations, which is constantly being transcended and partially destroyed, but which is always being reborn.[11]

Thus the relation of human beings and things is not simply a technical problem to be overcome through ingenuity; it is a profound structuring element introducing violence and non-humanity into human affairs.

The second totalisation (scarcity) is one form of the first totalisation (need). The determination of scarcity introduces matter into human relations as non-humanity. In the case of need, the non-humanity arose from within the activity of the individual, who made him or herself into a thing. Scarcity is one form that matter can take in shaping human relations. It pertains more directly to the way human beings interact than the case of need, which remained at the individual level. It demonstrates, in a way that the case of need does not, that social relations cannot be understood without considering the role of matter.

In an interesting discussion of the master-slave relation in Hegel, Sartre seeks to prove the importance of the concept of scarce matter. Hegel's *Phenomenology* presented one stage in the development of self-consciousness as a conflict between masters and slaves. The master was unable to achieve recognition of his humanity from the slave because ironically the slave was inhuman in the master's eyes. Since the slave did what the master commanded, the master was unable to obtain confirmation of his freedom from a being who was not free. The master, according to Hegel, has been constituted as such through a struggle to death with the other, who when vanquished, became the slave. The social relation of master to slave is constituted for Hegel out of the pure struggle for recognition between two consciousnesses. Sartre objects to Hegel's view of the master-slave relation because Hegel has failed to account for the role of scarce matter. Hegel is an idealist, Sartre contends, because the initial struggle between the master and slave was concerned only with the destruction of the other. Like Hobbes, Hegel posits two individuals in conflict. Because the conflict is an end in itself, Hegel mystifies human relations as inherently conflictual. When scarcity is taken into account, one can see that the struggle was not simply an honorific duel, but a means to create an institution in which scarcity would be diminished for the victor.[12]

Sartre also points out that Hegel confuses the issue by speaking of a single master and a single slave. For Hegel the master seeks recognition only from the slave. Hegel has thus omitted the class of masters and the role of other masters in the constitution of master consciousness. The master is not simply at an impasse, as Hegel would have it, failing to achieve recognition. He forms his consciousness instead from other masters who reinforce the ideology of the ruling class and imagine falsely that all masters are indeed human. Scarcity has produced a society of masters who justify the oppression of the slaves by imagining that humanity consists of being a master. The rulers of class society must justify their position by accounting for the interiorisation of matter as scarcity.

Human relations are totalised by matter in another set of ways which are distinct from the situation of scarcity. In addition to not being enough, matter is shaped or worked by human beings, absorbing their purposes and intentions. Sartre characterises matter as inertia and passivity in that it simply accepts or receives human praxis. Like wax that is made into a seal by the use of a tool, matter 'reflects the *doing* as pure *being-there*'.[13] The intentional praxis becomes inscribed in matter, transforming the living act into an inert, material fact. The apparent passivity of worked matter is deceptive, however, because the living continuity of praxis has been changed into a frozen, dead reality.

The change in the status of praxis which has become embodied in matter is the condition for alienation according to Sartre. He writes that 'The real foundations of alienation appear' when 'matter alienates in itself the action which works it, not because it is itself a force nor even because it is inertia, but because its inertia allows it to absorb the labour power of Others and turn it back against everyone.'[14] The praxis of an individual becomes alienated or made other than what it was when its inscription in matter confronts the praxis of other individuals. Once absorbed by matter free praxis can lose its original meaning and take on new ones.

Sartre illustrates this important characteristic of worked matter through the example of the deforestation of China. Looking at the landscape of China today one is struck by the absence of trees, an absence undoubtedly not noticed by the inhabitants since they are accustomed to it. The lack of trees, however, was produced through centuries of actions by the Chinese peasants. Ages ago, each peasant cleared his plot, reclaiming the forest for agriculture. The praxis of farming was inscribed in the land by the uprooting and removal of trees. In the days when the deforestation was carried out, everyone accepted the destruction of the trees for what it was: an attempt to make the land fertile. Yet the land has its revenge. Denuded of trees, it became subject to dangerous flooding, a condition that no one expected or desired. The meaning of the praxis of ground-clearing was altered. It became the opposite of what it had been. What was once an act of reclamation was now a condition of erosion, flooding, damage to farming. 'Thus the absence of trees', Sartre writes, 'which is an inert and thus a material negation, also has the systematic character of a *praxis* at the heart of materiality.'[15]

The original finality or intention of the peasants was alienated (made other) producing what Sartre terms 'counter-finality'. Through worked matter, alienation is introduced into the social field in the form of counter-finality. This process is 'anti-dialectical', to use another Sartrean term, in that the intelligibility of individual praxis is reversed: matter creates needs for human beings. Yet the example of the deforestation of China introduces only one form of the relation in which worked matter acts upon human beings. In Sartre's words, 'This first relation of man to the non-human — where Nature becomes the negation of man precisely to the extent that man is made *anti-physis* and that the actions in exteriority of the atomised masses are united by the communal character of their results – does not as yet integrate materiality with the social, but makes mere Nature, as a brutal, exterior limitation of society, into the unity of men.'[16]

Sartre provides a second example of the effects of worked matter on human praxis which accounts for the case of the social character of matter. Spain in the sixteenth century pursued a policy of bringing back gold and silver from the new world. These precious metals, examples of worked matter, were symbolic of the power of imperial Spain. Yet as quickly as the coins were brought into Spain, they flowed out of it into the coffers of European monarchs. Worked matter embodied the praxis of the Spaniards and indicated their wealth. At the same time, it negated this praxis and redefined it as poverty. The solidarity of the Spanish ruling class, the reciprocal recognition of each as pursuing the project of wealth and power, was undermined by the outflow of gold, transforming their relations into hostile, non-human otherness. Sartre sums up the process as follows:

> Precious metal presented itself as *the* wealth of Spain, that is to say, it appeared, through the legal activities of merchants and of the government, as a material synthetic power liable both to increase and to decrease. Thus the losses of gold were regarded by the Cortes *as a systematic impoverishment* of the country. The unity of the concerted process of accumulation gave matter its passive unity as wealth; and this material unity in its turn unified the amorphous growth in fraud and in imports. In this way, matter itself became the essential thing, and individuals disappeared unrecognised into inessentiality. What had to be stopped was the *outflow of gold*.[17]

This example demonstrates the way matter can take precedence over people, alienating the meanings of individual and collective actions so that the recognition of human beings as human is lost in favour of the priority of the thing. Social relations are 'shot through with passivity' and therefore with alienation as matter twists and transforms the dialectic of praxis. The name Sartre gives to matter which has absorbed the past actions and meanings of human beings is the practico-inert. The dialectical formula that human beings mediate things to the extent that things mediate human beings becomes a world of alienation under the impact of the practico-inert. In short, 'at any moment of History things are human precisely to the extent that men are things'.[18]

Sartre's explanation of alienation through the effects of the practico-inert appear to differ considerably from that of Marx and many commentators have criticised Sartre accordingly. More sharply than anyone else, Pietro Chiodi has argued that Sartre's definition of alienation is incompatible with marxism. He contends that for Sartre, 'dispersion in . . . objectivity . . . is always identified with alienation [and] overcoming alienation is a magico-idealistic aspiration for flight from this worldly dispersion towards retreat in the nostalgia of original subjectivity'.[19] Chiodi's criticism can be answered only by looking closely at the definitions of alienation in Hegel, Marx and Sartre.

Hegel identified alienation with objectification. To the extent that an individual was not identical with himself he was alienated. In thought or action, the individual separated his concept from himself bringing it into the outside world. For Hegel therefore all action was alienating. In his effort to generate categories adequate for the critique of capitalism, Marx differed from Hegel by distinguishing between alienation and objectification. Alienation was limited to specific forms of objectification, those in which the object became lost from the individual and took on 'alien' meanings. Ordinarily objectification did not represent a loss, according to Marx. Man was a 'natural' being and as such had needs that bound him to the objective world. In Marx's account, man himself was an objective being whose actions were rooted in the world. With his idealistic presuppositions Hegel regarded man as a purely subjective being for whom objectivity represented degradation. The distinction between alienation and objectification enabled Marx to present a critique of the capitalist mode of production. Under capitalism the praxis of the worker was alienated because the product of labour, the process of labour and the relations between labourers were all under the control of the capitalist. A mode of production without alienation (communism) was possible since the workers could recapture their lost praxis by appropriating the product and process of labour. Such an appropriation would not mean, it must be pointed out, that labour would lose its character as objectification. Workers would still act upon the world in collective structures, employing their energy to fashion products.

Sartre compares his definition of alienation with those of Hegel and Marx in a passage that is worth quoting at length:

> The man who looks at his work, who recognises himself in it completely, and who also does not recognise himself in it at all; the man who can say both: 'This is not what I wanted' and 'I understand that this is what I have done and that I could not do anything else', and whose free *praxis* refers him to his prefabricated being and who recognises himself equally in both – this man grasps, in an immediate dialectical movement, necessity as the *destiny in exteriority of freedom*.
>
> Should we describe this as alienation? Obviously we should, in that *he returns to himself as Other*. However, a distinction must be made: alienation in the marxist sense begins with exploitation. Should we go back to Hegel who sees alienation as a constant characteristic of all kinds of objectification? Yes and no. We must recognise that the original relation between *praxis* as totalisation and materiality as passivity obliges man to objectify himself in a milieu which is not his own, and to treat an inorganic totality as his own objective reality. It is this relation between interiority and exteriority which originally constituted *praxis* as a relation of the organism to its material environment; and there can be no doubt that as soon as man begins to designate himself not as the mere reproduction of his life, but as the ensemble of products which reproduce his life, he discovers himself as *Other* in the world of objectivity; totalised matter, as inert objectification perpetuated by inertia, is in effect *non-human* or even *anti-human*. All of us spend our lives engraving our maleficent image on things, and it fascinates and bewilders us if we try to understand ourselves *through it*, although we are ourselves the totalising movement which results in this particular objectification.[20]

Chiodi refers to this passage as proof of his case against Sartre.

Sartre appears to agree with Hegel that alienation is a matter of a self becoming other when it objectifies itself. But there is a difference. While Sartre does indeed define alienation in terms of making the self other, thereby placing the emphasis on the subjective state of the individual, he does so in the context of generating categories for making intelligible a limited portion of human experience, that is, 'history'. This 'history' is confined to the project of overcoming scarcity. Within the context of scarcity, matter structures praxis in definite ways, which have been outlined. For Sartre, praxis in the context of scarcity is necessarily alienating because the anti-dialectic has penetrated human relations. Therefore, while it is true that Sartre shifts the locus of alienation away from the context of capitalist exploitation, he has not identified simple objectification with alienation. Objectification is alienating, for Sartre, in the context of 'history' *only*. The *Critique* does not argue, as Chiodi contends, that dispersion in the world is itself alienating. It does argue, however, that alienation is a broader concept than it is in Marx.

The difference between the concepts of alienation in Sartre and Marx is not that Sartre has retreated into hegelian idealism but that he has expanded the domain of the concept to include all effects of the practico-inert. The question to be asked therefore is whether Sartre's concept of alienation enables marxism to account for modes of alienation which hitherto it has ignored.

Marx limits alienation closely to the realm of labour. The *1844 Manuscripts* present a trenchant critique of capitalism only in terms of alienated labour. But nowhere does Marx justify this limitation. There is a strong tendency in Marx, however, to restrict the scope of praxis to labour. The act of labour is the centre of all social action for Marx. Labour is a mirror through which the multiplicity of social behaviour is reflected. The status of the proletariat as the *universal* class is derived from its position in the structure of work. Marx argues that the radical chains of the working class are forged by the anvil of alienated labour. Unlike other oppressed classes in history —

slaves, serfs, artisans, and so forth – the proletariat is unique in its universality. Its misery is the key, for Marx, to the complete emancipation of humanity.

> A class must be formed which has *radical chains*, a class in civil society which is not a class of civil society, a class which is the dissolution of all classes, a sphere of society which has a universal character because its sufferings are universal, and which does not claim a *particular redress* because the wrong which is done to it is not a *particular wrong* but *wrong in general*. . . . This dissolution of society, as a particular class, is the *proletariat*.[21]

Marx is incorrect in arguing that overcoming alienated labour is identical with human emancipation. Women and children, for example, suffer forms of domination in which the male working class participates and even enjoys. By restricting the concept of alienation to the labour situation marxism ignores other modes of oppression the abolition of which is crucial for 'human emancipation'. It can be argued that Sartre's expansion of the concept of alienation to the practico-inert in general provides a superior basis for critical theory to that of Marx. If Sartre's concept of alienation were no more than a complaint about otherness, a protest against the individual's non-identity, it would be useless for marxism. Since his concept of alienation is rather an attempt to make intelligible all the forms through which praxis becomes lost and opposed to its creators, Sartre has introduced into marxism a deeper comprehension of social misery. The connection between the practico-inert and alienation enables the critical historian to explore the multitudinous forms that inhumanity has taken in the process of overcoming scarcity. Sartre's contention deserves serious consideration: human beings have been alienated not only by the capitalist organisation of labour but by all actions which introduce into human affairs the counter-finality of the practico-inert.

An example of the complex relation between alienation and the practico-inert is found in the concept of class or individual interest. Both liberal and socialist theory commonly employ the notion of interest in ways that, according to Sartre, obscure the mediation of human beings by things. Marxists often write of the class interest of the proletariat as if that interest is an unmediated expression of the revolutionary situation. Situated in an exploitative position in the capitalist mode of production, the workers' interest is quite naturally the overthrow of the system. From Sartre's point of view, on the contrary, the interest of the workers is already an alienated expression of their relation to worked matter. He defines interest as

> the inorganic materiality of the individual or group seen as an absolute and irreducible being which subordinates itself to *praxis* as a way of preserving itself in its practico-inert exteriority. In other words, it is the passive, inverted image of freedom, and the only way in which freedom can produce itself (and become conscious of itself) in the shifting hell of the field of practical passivity.[22]

Interest expressed freedom, but only after the workers' consciousness has been distorted by worked matter.

According to Marx the workers' interest lies in reappropriating the machines that are their alienated labour. But, Sartre writes, '. . . the machine could *never* be the particular interest of the worker'.[23] As embodiments of alienated labour, the machine is the worker as otherness. When the worker sees his interest and freedom in the machine, that interest has already been misshaped by scarce matter. The real freedom of the worker must lie beyond his interest in the machine. Sartre states the problem in the clearest terms:

> The contradiction of interest is that it reveals itself in the individual or collective attempt to rediscover the original univocal bond between man and matter, that is to say, free constituent *praxis*, but that it is already in itself the perversion and petrification of this attempt by matter as the false counterpart of human action.[24]

The interest of the worker in socialising the means of production reflects the complexity of alienation through the practico-inert more than it does the transcendence of scarcity.

In the alienated world of capitalism, interests are in conflict. Indeed, they are an expression of conflict. One cannot therefore see them as the basis for a society without class conflict. Interest presupposes conflict over scarce matter. It cannot capture the image of a world beyond alienation. For Sartre, interests are not revolutionary.

> There is a choice: either 'everyone follows his interest', which implies that divisions between men are *natural* – or it is divisions between men, resulting from the mode of production, which make interest (particular or general, individual or class) appear as a real moment of the relations between men.[25]

Sartre's critique of the notion of interest does not imply a fall into utopianism. Simply because class interest is intertwined with alienation one cannot conclude that socialism will cause the immediate and total disappearance of interest. The struggle to overthrow capitalism will be based neither upon the 'natural interest' of the workers nor upon some pure revolutionary will. Sartre is careful to allow for the continuation of forms of alienation in post-revolutionary society.

> This does not mean that a real socialisation of the means of production must, in a particular historical development, lead to the total elimination of interest itself as linking men in *alterity* through matter. On the contrary, interest *arises*, as always, out of *alterity* as the primary human practical relation, but as deformed by the matter which mediates it; and it maintains itself in the milieu of alterity.[26]

Sartre's awareness of the difficulty in overcoming scarcity, however, does not compel him to hypostasise scarcity and interest as the inevitable fate of mankind. The transcendental deduction of the categories of dialectical reason, let us recall, does not flirt with atemporal truths. Concerning the persistence of interests under socialism, Sartre writes, 'The whole of my description here applies, really, to the first stages of capitalism (the existence of activist groups and of workers' institutions, as well as the achievement of socialism in certain countries, completely transforms the problem).[27]

The discussion of interest as a form of alienation in relations between human beings leads Sartre to the exposition of one of his most important categories, that is, seriality. In the case of interest, as in all relations mediated by the practico-inert, matter (the machine) introduces passivity into human relations. People become other than themselves, incorporating as their own the exteriority and the inertness of worked matter. The worker is separated from the boss by the struggle over the control of the machine, just as the workers are separated from each other. As the focus of the unity of human beings, matter can, in Sartre's words, 'only be their separation'. Yet, as Sartre points out, this separation is lived by people and interiorised. The otherness of matter becomes, in the context of common praxis, 'a bond of lived interiority'. If, as Marx writes of the commodity, reification remains the *appearance* of human beings becoming things, the task of social-historical analysis, indeed of revolution, would be considerably lightened. The problem is that the 'appearance' becomes the 'reality', a much more intransigent phenomenon to make intelligible and to struggle against.

When scarce matter forms the interior bond between people there is constituted a form of human relations that Sartre calls the series. In the series, people have internalised the passivity of the practico-inert and have become other than themselves. Incorporating the externality of matter, they then relate to each other as other than themselves. Since people in series are not pure material objects, but subjects who regard themselves and others as objects, the description of this mediation is necessarily complicated. Sartre explains the difference between the series and objects as follows:

> In fact the quantitative relations between physical molecules are radically different from the relations between social atoms. The former act and react in the milieu of exteriority; the latter in that of interiority. Everyone determines both himself and the Other in so far as he is Other than the Other and Other than himself.[28]

The obscurity of the series is clarified considerably by Sartre through an example of a group of people waiting for a bus. Sartre describes the situation in which there is

> a group of people waiting for a bus, in which none of them pays the slightest attention to the others — all eyes are turned towards the rue

de Rennes, looking out for the bus which is about to arrive. In this state of semi-isolation, it is obvious that they are united by the street, the square, the paving-stones and the asphalt, the pedestrian crossings, and the bus, that is to say, by the material underside of a passivised *praxis*.[29]

Here is a not uncommon case of human beings relating to each other through the mediation of worked matter, the bus. Because they are human beings, the relation is interior; there is a bond of humanity linking each to each. What is the nature of this bond?

The attention of the people in the queue is directed to the absent bus. Each has a common consciousness, anticipating the thing. Not only are they a group of people in the same location, who have recognised their community by forming themselves into a line, but they have the same intention, the same consciousness. The bond of each to each is one of discrete, separate identity. Each in his individuality, in his waiting for the bus, is like the others. They are the same only through their bond with the thing. The schedule of the bus and its route are the occasion through which they have come together. The materialised praxis of the public transportation system has constituted them as a temporary community.

Although the lives of the group do not seem to be bound together profoundly, because they are human the experience could be fateful for all. There could be an accident, or a robbery; they could get caught in a prolonged traffic jam or in a protest movement. Any of these eventualities could lead to an extended relationship among the passengers. The lives of any or all of the group could be affected drastically by the experience. Friendships could be formed; love could blossom. But let us suppose that none of this happens. Instead the example provides only an ordinary, everyday experience of life in Paris.

Perhaps there will not be enough seats. In this case, the bond of each person in the line to the others becomes a question of privilege and competition. Each views the other as one who might take the last seat, forcing them to stand and be uncomfortable, even though the fare was the same for all. Hence each person views the other as

68

another body to occupy a seat. Scarcity has entered the group, determining relations between individuals as that of hostile competition. The other is not recognised for his or her humanity but for being a body who can take up a seat. Each is interchangeable for the others, an identical atom whose individuality and humanity are negated. Each is therefore other than him or herself, penetrated by materiality, for the others. It is only because that person is other than this person that this person maintains a bond with that person. 'In the series', Sartre writes, 'everyone becomes himself (*as Other than self*) in so far as he is other than the Others, and in so far as the Others are other than him.'[30]

Capturing a ubiquitous experience, the series illustrates the scandalous quality of relations mediated by things. The thing takes precedence over human beings, deflecting their consciousness from mutual recognition and transforming reciprocity into bonds of exteriority. People have become things to each other and each must endure this obnoxious fact. The emphasis in Sartre's concept of seriality falls not on the appearance of reification but on the existential quality of the relation between things:

> The serial movement in our example excludes the relation of reciprocity: everyone is the Reason for the Other-Being of the Other in so far as an Other is the reason for his being. In a sense, we are back with material exteriority, which should come as no surprise since the series is determined by inorganic matter. On the other hand, to the extent that the ordering was performed *by some practice*, and that this practice included reciprocity within it, it contains a *real interiority*.[31]

Sartre provides other examples of the series — listening to a radio broadcast, reading a newspaper, buying a commodity on a market. In some cases individuals are physically dispersed; in others they act in proximity. The essential point does not change: each atom in the social totality acts the same way; the action is shaped by a material object; the interior bond between individuals internalises the inertness of matter. In the case of behaviour on a market, the serial quality of the experience belies the promise of freedom. In liberal theory, the independent act of buying and selling confirms the freedom of capitalism. The quintessence of rationality and autonomy, market behaviour, according to classical liberalism, is the epitome of our humanity. Such optimism is not warranted from the perspective of the concept of the series.

When an individual makes a purchase, there is a presumption that countless others are doing the same. The price of an item is determined by the quantity of purchases and the availability of the item. Each individual therefore presumes that there are others who are acting like themselves and that these actions have a great deal to do with how they will act. If too many people want the same product the price will rise, perhaps putting it out of reach. The bond between people, which liberalism characterises as freedom, is in fact penetrated by inhumanity, with each considering the other a threat and an enemy. Sartre explains the serial quality of market relations as follows:

> Everyone's expectations, in a market that is supposed to be competitive, depends on the hypothesis that atomisation will remain the typical social link at least for the duration of the exchange. Thus, the unity cannot be conceived as a unifying synthesis, but as a form of dispersal as such, when this dispersal is seen as a rule and means for action.[32]

In Sartre's view market relations do more than reify and obscure the productive power of the workers. They go beyond that, forming a curious bond between people which alienates them from each other in a manner overlooked by marxists. Since market relations form an ongoing practice for members of industrial society, they cannot be relegated to the status of epiphenomena. They constitute rather a major aspect of social life and need to be made intelligible as such. Dialectical reason reveals the series as a prominent component of historical experience. The series is the most characteristic form of praxis in a world where things take precedence over human beings in shaping human relations.

Although atomisation is the most obvious example of the

series there are serial situations in which individuals appear to be bound together tightly in a mass. The example of this case presented by Sartre is the 'great fear' which occurred during the French Revolution of 1789. In the heated atmosphere of the revolution, peasants all over France armed themselves and kept the vigil for bands of vagabonds, aristocrats, brigands, who, they imagined, were bent on destruction. There was, in Georges Lefebvre's phrase, a rural panic of major proportions.[33] Those opposed to the revolution attributed the great fear to the manipulations of the revolutionary government, frightening the peasants into violence against the nobility. Lefebvre disagrees, arguing that the fear was a spontaneous outburst which can be 'explained by the economic, social and political circumstances prevailing in France in 1789'.[34]

Sartre, in turn, rejects Lefebvre's mode of explanation in favour of one which relies on the concept of seriality. One needs to show how the peasants constituted that group of roving vagabonds as Other. He continues,

> Neither the economic, political and social causes known to us, nor the fear of bandits or the constitution *of the milieu of the Other* as a refracting medium (*milieu*) of History are enough to explain the Great Fear. . . . The Great Fear . . . had to be triggered off by some local incident which was perceived as Other by those who witnessed it, and seriality had to propagate itself by becoming *actualized*.[35]

Beyond the question of economic and political conditions, the historian has to show how the peasants totalised the situation, how they constituted the Other in the realm of seriality. Each peasant constituted himself as the Other who was threatened by the roving bands. Resorting to social conditions for an explanation does not account for the subjective factor of the extraordinary change in the peasants' consciousness. Only the concept of the series can describe it.

The case of the great fear serves as an illustration, for Sartre, of the workings of public opinion in general. It exemplifies the way in which certain notions spread like a contagion across society when there appears to be little rational basis or firm evidence for them. The mild mass hysteria of UFO reportings might be cited as such a phenomenon. In cases like this each citizen identifies with another who has made a report. The individual is not an active agent but a passive target of some dangerous force. Public opinion is founded on what Sartre calls 'human impotence'. 'The *opinions* of public opinion arise like the Great Fear, in that everyone makes himself Other by his opinion, that is to say, by taking it *from the Other* because the Other believes it as Other, and makes himself the informer of the Others.'[36] Only the distance between people constituted as a series can account for the phenomenon of public opinion.

No less than public opinion, the concept of the series informs the basic category of marxism, that is, class. Marx defined class as the relation of a group to the means of production. This concept of class is purely structural or objective. It is not a matter of the perceptions of the group. Factory workers in the United States might think of themselves as middle class, yet they remain, for Marx, proletarians. Marx supplemented the notion of class with that of class consciousness, that is, the awareness of oneself as positioned in a social structure at a certain point. Those members of a class who do not perceive themselves, who do not constitute their world view and political activity in correspondence with their relation to the means of production suffer what Marx termed false consciousness.

These traditional categories of marxism capture only weakly the relationship between consciousness and society. Marxist theory orients historical analysis towards the mode of production and its relations with politics. It is not an adequate instrument for explaining subtle shifts in consciousness or even for grasping major changes in group consciousness. When a group is radicalised, marxists explain the change most often by referring to aspects of the social and political conjuncture. Sartre's treatment of the concept of class is intended to remedy this deficiency in marxist theory. For Sartre, in the final analysis, one makes oneself a bourgeois or a proletarian. Class is more than a set of objective characteristics; it is lived experience, a mode of totalising one's world, and it requires a complex set of categories to render it intelligible.

Sartre develops his notion of class-being in conjunction with his concept of the practico-inert. The attribute of class situates a person in an ensemble of material objects. The means of production – machines, practices, buildings, and so forth – become for him a complex of worked matter. Class-being then is a designation one has because of one's relation to the practico-inert. Sartre writes,

> I am referring to *inert collective being*, as the *inorganic common materiality* of all the members of a given ensemble. This indeed is basically what it means to speak of a class. For the term does not primarily mean either the active unification of all the individuals within the organisations which they themselves have produced, or an identity of nature between several separate products.[37]

Membership in a class inserts one in a particular relation to worked matter.

In this sense, class-being does not imply political activity. The emphasis in Sartre's concept of class falls on the inertness of the status, the way in which it defines the individual in relation to things and as a thing. Indeed for Sartre class-being, far from a staging-point of revolution, is a mark of serial passivity. Situated in a class, the individual interiorises a certain relation to the world in which things form the active element. Workers and bourgeois alike, in so far as they are determined by class, are pervaded by otherness or alterity. Sartre goes so far as to account for the passivity of the French working class in the nineteenth century, its lack of revolutionary militance, by its class-being. 'What made the workers impotent, in the first half of the last century, was alterity as spatial and temporal stratification.'[38] Certain characteristics of the French class structure encouraged not struggle but quietism. In the most explicit terms Sartre denies that class-being leads to revolution: 'the practical unity of men can never arise or originate in the domination of worked matter over man'.[39]

Granted this grim argument, Sartre nevertheless affirms the revolutionary character of the working class. The crucial point for him is not that class-being is revolutionary, but that workers, in spite of their class status, in spite of their serial character, raise the arm of revolution to affirm their humanity: 'what finally characterises the working class . . . is that the organised *praxis* of a militant group originates in the very heart of the practico-inert, in the opaque materiality of impotence and inertia as a transcendence of this materiality'.[40] What traditional marxism failed to account for and to stress is that revolutionary struggle is conducted against the condition of being a worker. It is not because one is a worker that one rebels, but precisely because being a worker, being immersed in the series, is such a violation of free praxis that it must be destroyed as a social determination. Because the discussion in this chapter is limited to the force of matter over human beings, the categories for making intelligible revolutionary consciousness will not be presented here. It is enough at this point to underscore Sartre's insistence that class-being falls under the dead hand of the series.

In relation to the practico-inert freedom is restricted to the interiorisation of matter. Dialectical reason comprehends the mediation of matter not as a form of determinism, not as the external force of atom upon atom, but as the free praxis of passivity. Sartre insists that the exploration of relations in which matter predominates over human beings does not lead to the disappearance of freedom. Quite the contrary. 'In other words, freedom, in this context, does not mean the possibility of choice, but the necessity of living these constraints in the form of exigencies which must be fulfilled by a *praxis*.'[41] The capacity of human beings to totalise the social field does not vanish with the series. It takes on the character of alienation.

Sartre's presentation of the role of matter as a mediator of human relations differs in many regards from traditional marxism. In general, Sartre, far more than Marx, emphasises the subjective structures of alienation brought about by worked matter. As far as it goes, this direction is well taken because it enables dialectical reason to raise questions that hitherto have remained obscure in marxist thought. The underlying thread of Sartre's concepts is of course the problem of class consciousness. The *Critique* enables historical materialism to make intelligible an important dimension of the class struggle. The construction of socialism can now be understood not simply as the substitution of one mode of production for another, nor in terms of the political aspects of the class struggle. The question proposed by Sartre explores the new forms of consciousness required for a mode of production that is qualitatively different from capitalism. Socialism must overcome scarcity and the myriad forms it has taken in the practico-inert. Socialism must make possible a new relation between human beings and things, one in which the reciprocity of human beings would not be distorted by the inertness of matter. In sum, the construction of socialism demands a transformation of subjectivity as much as it does a change in objective structures.

There are serious inadequacies, however, in Sartre's conceptualisation of the role of matter. In the first place, the concept of matter as inert, inorganic, passive externality is much too flat and undifferentiated. It does not account for the difference between machines and buildings on the one hand and social institutions, patterned ways of behaviour, laws, norms and rules on the other. For Sartre it is all the same. In addition Sartre virtually ignores nature, leaving the implication that minerals and rocks, plant life and animals are all nothing but variations of inert, passive matter. Machines and herds of cows apparently have the same practico-inert status. The question of ecology is thus completely suppressed. At a time when industrial society is able to disrupt the eco-system — destroying whole species, threatening life itself with nuclear catastrophe — the concept of nature becomes paramount for social theory. Important political groups are forming in France more than elsewhere around the question of ecology. Perhaps they are not inherently opposed to marxism, but their politics differ considerably from a philosophy that proposes to conquer nature and sees history as scarcity. Ecological theory raises the question of the integration of society and nature as well as that of the appropriate level of needs that allow this balance. Like Marx, Sartre can offer little to those who are questioning the traditional model of abundance.[42]

Another serious weakness in Sartre's concept of matter derives from its alienating, regressive nature. Marx applauded capitalism for developing technology, for creating an expanding economic system which could generate material abundance as well as minimise human toil. Socialism, he thought, would complete the bourgeois project by automating the economy, thereby inaugurating the realm of freedom, of life beyond labour. For Sartre, on the contrary, the practico-inert can play no such role. At best matter is the occasion for freedom. Sartre writes, 'It is *the material object* which, by its mediation, *sets reciprocity free.*'[43] By this he means that the practico-inert is the context in which free projects are totalised. Such a view does not enable one to account for the progressive role of matter. Even in a negative sense, matter can be liberating because it can generate contradictions which inspire the class struggle. In marxism, the discontinuity between the means of production and the relations of production constitute a revolutionary situation. The collapse of capitalism, as in the depression of 1929, is part of the class struggle. The marxist view differs from liberal progressivism which recounts the onward march of science and technology. Nevertheless, the objective level of the practico-inert, for marxism, is a 'moment' of revolutionary emancipation. It can point towards liberation, whereas for Sartre it appears as a threat (in the case of the deforestation of China) or as a deadening weight upon reciprocity (in the case of the bus). Thus matter, in Sartre's hands, is removed from the context of historical change. It becomes almost a constant, an unchanging negation of reciprocity.

If matter appears as an ahistorical constant in the *Critique*, so the mediations of matter (worked matter, the practico-inert, the series, and other categories which there has not been space to discuss) are inadequately conceptualised. The series, for example, is always the same. The individual in the series is always other to the other. Alterity and alienation plague the serial individual regardless of the context. Within the boundaries of history such as Sartre defines it the series does not vary. Changing modes of production and political systems do not alter its basic structure. Under feudalism or capitalism or the transition from one to the other the series introduces the same externality and passivity into human relations. Hence the relationship between the traditional categories of historical materialism — the mode of production — is not integrated into Sartre's account. Aside from the revision of the concept of class, the *Critique* does not challenge the basic concepts of marxism. In places Sartre simply asserts the validity of the concept of the mode of production. However, the concepts of the practico-inert and the series would appear to have a direct impact on the way the mode of production is conceived, an impact that is left unexplored.

If the series is a flat, unchanging essence, standing aside from the mode of production, the cause may rest with Sartre's phenomenological-existential approach to social theory. Regardless of the validity of Sartre's reconstruction of the subject-object dialectic, he restricts the comprehension of the internal complexity of the practico-inert. The practico-inert consists of sedimentations of meanings and actions from the past. Its effect on the social field is limited to presenting a network of meanings which must be interiorised by totalising individuals and groups. The interplay or mediations between past praxis absorbed by matter and present praxis acting upon the world is made intelligible with great subtlety by Sartre. There is, however, another level of intelligibility to the practico-inert which Sartre does not reach. Institutions need to be comprehended apart from the way they absorb actions and are interiorised by social agents.[44]

Language, for example, has been analysed by structuralists in a manner that reveals an internal set of oppositions. These formal relationships connect each part of language to the whole so that it forms a system. This system in turn cannot be grasped in terms of a phenomenology of speech acts. The structure of language is epistemologically discontinuous with the intentions of speakers. It must be constructed by analysing language as if it were a thing, separate from the investigator and the social participant. Structuralists have also analysed kinship systems along the same lines and Althusser has presented a parallel interpretation of the marxist concept of the mode of production.

In *Capital* Marx probes the internal complexity of political economy. At times he discusses the effects of the system on the working class and their response to it; such presentations are commensurate with Sartre's method. At other times, however, Marx unveils the mechanism of capitalism, and even changes from one mode of production to another, without recourse to class struggle, praxis, or intentionality. Marx explores the change from the guild system to capitalism via the system of 'manufacture' without reference to historical subjects. He indicates that in one system a certain relation between capital, labour and tools obtains and that in another system the relations are altered.[45] Although such an analysis is by no means complete, Marx being the first who would call for a discussion of the class struggle in the course of the changes, it would be impossible to comprehend the role of praxis without first grasping the relations of the elements in each system.

Sartre does admit a role for what he calls analytical reason, that form of thought which treats society as a system of objects and breaks it down into its component parts. Marx's analysis of the change from manufacturing to capitalism might fit under the designation analytical reason. But Sartre does not acknowledge the importance to dialectical reason of the level of the internal complexity of objective systems. It becomes impossible for him therefore to judge whether a given set of individuals in a social field has comprehended fully the practico-inert against which they act. Sartre can discriminate praxis that aims at the overthrow of seriality from that which does not. But he cannot distinguish between politics that is revolutionary in relation to a mode of production, or even in relation to a political system, from that which is not because he has no way to estimate what the mode of production is. For example, Sartre cannot decide between the politics of anarchists like Proudhon and socialists like Marx in the period after 1848 because he cannot illuminate which group comprehended better the system they both wanted to overthrow. Certainly he can distinguish between projects and totalisations; he can make intelligible the way each group, anarchists and socialists, struggled against seriality and the problems that beset Europe at that time. But Sartre's method, based on the categories developed in the *Critique* for the comprehension of relations between human beings and things in which things predominate, cannot satisfy its own criteria of moving history towards a single totalisation since it cannot speak about the nature of the social machine in terms of which the totalisation must rebel.

As a final criticism of this section of the *Critique* the question of Sartre's individualism must be raised again. Earlier it was argued that criticisms of Sartre's position based on the charge of individualism were inadequate. After reviewing the concepts of the practico-inert and seriality we can see more clearly why this is so. Sartre employed the notion of individual praxis as a framework for approaching the question of relations between human beings and things. That did not prevent him from conceptualising group praxis, or from making intelligible relations between people in the series. Thus the concept of individual praxis did not operate the way the notion of individualism does in the liberal tradition of social theory. Individual praxis is not for Sartre a pre-social concept which renders society epiphenomenal and leads to a concept of natural rights on the one hand or to the antinomies of freedom/determinism on the other.

Nevertheless, Sartre's use of the concept of individual praxis does at times detract from his social theory. Instead of being a mediating concept which is valid only for the generation of social categories, the concept of individual praxis in some places is ontologised and contradicts the project of the *Critique*. Sartre incants a dangerous refrain repeatedly: 'the only practical dialectical reality, the motive force of everything, *is individual action*'.[46] And again:

> *The entire historical dialectic rests on individual praxis in so far as it is already dialectical*, that is to say, to the extent that action is itself the negating transcendence of contradiction, the determination of a present totalisation in the name of a future totality, and the real effective working of matter.[47]

Finally, 'The only concrete basis for the historical dialectic is the dialectical structure of individual action.'[48] These citations could be multiplied at will. The problem they raise, however, puts in doubt the advances of Sartre's position.

The purpose of the *Critique* is to test the validity of dialectical reason whose domain is history. If this is so, then the primary object that needs to be illuminated is the class struggle and the possibility of socialism. However detailed the analysis, dialectical reason always moves from the standpoint of the future of socialism. It is concerned with social forms and their limits, group behaviour and its alienation, institutions and their types of oppression. For the most part Sartre's *Critique* addresses itself to these questions. To a certain extent, however, Sartre's insistence on the primacy of the individual puts obstacles in the path of that goal. The more he repeats that dialectical reality is restricted to 'individual action', that history rests on 'individual praxis', the more he confuses and obscures the nature of historical materialism. The more the individual is placed in the forefront of the dialectic, the less the questions of social transformation are pertinent. There is a tendency in Sartre's text – it is only a tendency but it exists none the less – to privilege individual reality over social experience. While it remains possible, indeed it is necessary, to move, in Sartre's terms, from the individual to the totality, it is not clear why this movement is the centrepiece of analysis. One effect Sartre's reliance on the concept of individual praxis has certainly had is to mislead his readers into perceiving his position along traditional liberal and existentialist lines. Statements such as the individual is 'the motive force of everything' are, to say the least, obfuscating. Since only individuals in groups can transform social systems, Sartre's phrase detracts from his theory. The conclusion one is forced to draw is that elements of earlier positions persist in the *Critique*; but while they certainly warrant criticism they do not undermine the central theses of Sartre's marxism.

4. Groups, Organisations and Institutions

In the context of series and collectives, where the mediation of the practico-inert is decisive, a new form of praxis arises whose intelligibility rests more on human freedom than on material inertia. Groups are constituted within series and against them. They are structured by bonds of reciprocity which overcome passivity, alterity, alienation – all the modes of inhumanity that weigh upon history. Sartre's concept of the group explores those historical situations in which oppressed classes struggle against domination. It conceptualises especially changes in consciousness that occur during moments of revolutionary action. Sartre's intention is to make available to historical materialism a means of studying the subjective side of social change.

Sartre begins his discussion of the group by examining the conditions under which it arises. The example he uses for illustration is the storming of the Bastille during the opening phase of the French revolution of 1789. Early in July, while the national assembly was meeting, Paris had not yet changed. People lived in series and collectives as they had before. On the 12th posters announced the movement of troops around Paris, allegedly to protect the city from bandits. The rumour spread quickly that the troops surrounded Paris for a different reason: to suppress the revolution and perhaps attack the city. People began to see things in a new light. The other was no longer simple alterity. The other was in danger like myself. The other was me. Sartre outlines the change: 'everyone continued to see himself in the Other, but saw himself there as *himself* . . . everyone sees his own future in the other.'[1] The distance that separated people through the mediation of the practico-inert was beginning to vanish.

People began to talk and act together. Dotting the streets of

Paris, groups gathered in fear and anticipation. Some began to arm themselves; arsenals were looted. Groups reformed and talked about what was to be done. Inexorably and without deliberate plans people were forming into groups. The historical temperature was rising. Suddenly normal routines no longer seemed as important. The focus everywhere was on the troops and the danger they represented. Total strangers now had a common interest, a common concern, indeed, a common fate. The tempo increased. Speeches were being made, information was circulated. The necessity of alienation and atomisation had to be undone. Solidarity was urgent. People had to be trusted and action in concert, for no pay, at no one's orders, without customary sanctions, was mandatory.

In the Saint-Antoine district the Bastille had long represented the Old Regime. The fortress stood there unmoved by the poverty and wretchedness surrounding it. If only a handful of prisoners remained sequestered in the Bastille it none the less symbolised the established order. What was more it held weapons. So the fortress drew people to it, like metal filings to a magnet, people who, more and more desperately, more and more passionately, wanted the arms it contained. As the gates were opened and the surrender of the Bastille announced, a new form of human society, a new structure of relations had emerged in the streets.

The new group – Sartre calls it a fused group – had been shaped by the practico-inert, but only to a limited extent. Like the bus in the example of the series, the Bastille served as a material focus of people's consciousness. Sartre insists that the fused group depends on worked matter; it does not emerge anywhere but in the context of scarcity. 'The important point as far as the genesis of an active group is concerned, is that [the practico-inert] *actually* structured a route. . . . And this route was negative: it was the opportunity for troops to enter the district.'[2] The group is formed 'under the pressure of definite material circumstances'.[3] But none of this was new: there was always worked matter; the street could always be used by troops; the Bastille always had arms. The negative role of matter, presenting a threat to the existence of a group, is a

82

condition necessary but not sufficient for the birth of a fused group.

There is another side to the role of matter in this process. Matter also presents itself as something that can be overcome, as the basis for a possible unity between people. Matter as an obstacle to be removed is the decisive structural condition for the group. Sartre writes,

> It is always possible for materiality, as worked Thing, to posit itself as essential through the inessentiality of separated men, and, in the seriality of inert-men, to constitute an imperceptible and omnipresent structure of free practical unity. Basically this means that scarcity itself, as a tension of the polyvalent practical field, at the same time as constituting man as the other species, determines, in the same field, an undifferentiated (valid for any kind of grouping) possibility of unifying synthesis.[4]

A partial answer then to the question why groups emerge is that the context of the practico-inert provides both a negative threat and a positive occasion for unity.

Although Sartre connects the formation of the group with material conditions he does not explain adequately why the formation takes place at a particular time. The conditions for the birth of a fused group always exist. The oppressed are always subject to threats from the ruling powers. Social contradictions always bear heavily on the underclass. The encirclement of Paris that was the occasion for the storming of the Bastille was only an accentuation of normal conditions of life under the Old Regime. In fact, things were often worse. Peasants and artisans continually suffered indignities that were far more violent than a movement of troops. Marxists are accustomed to more detailed and convincing accounts of the objective conditions of the revolution than Sartre provides.

Sartre's answer to the marxists goes back to the question of determinism. One cannot argue for direct causes of revolutionary action and at the same time claim that the action is free. If men are free to make revolution and if in their revolutionary action they actualise that freedom, such action cannot be 'explained' by resorting to 'objective factors'. The material conditions are always there; revolutions occur at specific times, not necessarily when the contradiction between forces and relations of production is greatest. Marxists should be concerned, Sartre responds, not with *explaining* freedom but with comprehending it and making it intelligible. Dialectical reason pursues the question of how people revolt not like that of how water boils, but in order to see how one can describe the structural changes in human relations that are born in free action. The discussion of the fused group must shift, therefore, from an account of its conditions to an exploration of its structure. The external threat has torn 'everyone away from his Other-Being', but it cannot account for the new reality.

The first aspect of the group's structure is that everyone has the project of overcoming scarcity. Sartre states this position time and again without ambiguity: 'The deepest origin of the group' is that it 'produces itself through the project of taking the inhuman power of mediation between men away from worked matter and giving it, in the community, to each and to all and constituting itself, as structured, as a resumption of control over the materiality of the practical field (things and collectives) by free *communised praxis*.'[5] The fused group is the project of dismantling the myriad of structures that arose within scarcity and bore that trace as the perpetuation of inhumanity. Thus the fused group acts against all social institutions – economy, state, family, etc. – to the extent that each embodies, in different ways and to different degrees, a form of alienation. In short, the fused group has the project of freedom.

The second aspect of the fused group derives from the first: everyone has the *same* project. In Sartre's words, 'the basis of intelligibility, for the fused group, is that the structure of certain objectives . . . is revealed through the *praxis* of the individual as demanding the common unity of a *praxis* which is everyone's.'[6] Sartre designates the fused group as a 'community' because it encompasses 'the individual discovery of common action as the sole means of reaching the common objective'.[7] The individual cannot fight the king's troops alone even though he is designated as a target of their bullets. When the individual recognises that he or she must join with others and that others are in the same condition and have the same project, the relation of the individual to others is transformed.

In the fused group the individual recognises in the other not an other but himself. He sees in the other his own project duplicated; he sees in the other an incarnation of his own project of freedom. The existence of the common project in the other confirms and gives substance to the individual's project. The notion of opposing the king is no longer an idle fantasy but an objective reality. Revolution is everywhere in the streets. A bond is formed, a bond of interiority which is based on mutual recognition. 'This internal, synthetic constitution of me by the group is simply totalisation returning to me to give me my first *common* quality over the collapse of seriality.'[8] The individual's free project is recognised and confirmed by the other. It is not just that the other has the same project as the individual. In the series, both have the project of taking the bus. Because the project is one of freedom, the other presents no threat to the individual. Hence the fused group presents a reorganisation of the bonds between people such that the interiority of freedom has become the exterior basis of common action.

Sartre's concept of the fused group overcomes considerably the criticism that freedom for him is individualistic. Although freedom is connected with the structure of individual action, and as such provides the basis for the intelligibility of dialectical reason, it is only completed in a fused group. In one sense for Sartre freedom is always there in the social field: the individual can always form a project to go beyond the situation. In another sense freedom is there in the social field only in the act of revolution since only then does freedom become the basic structure of the relations between people. The fused group is thus that structure in which freedom is manifested most completely. Yet there is no necessity that this incarnation of freedom prevail in history. The advantage of Sartre's concept of freedom is that it allows for indeterminacy and contingency. Always there is one sense, only there in the full sense at certain times, freedom becomes the telos of history without becoming its inexorable law. The fused group is a possibility of history, one that has been realised at certain times, but one that is not the inevitable outcome of evolutionary law. 'The essential characteristic of the fused group', then, 'is the sudden resurrection of freedom. Not that freedom ever ceased to be the very condition of acts and the mask which conceals alienation.'[9] Unlike orthodox marxists who see freedom as the rational interest of workers (or the party) who comprehend correctly the objective contradictions of the capitalist mode of production, Sartre views freedom as the upsurge of mutual recognition in the context of daily life.

How is it possible, critics have asked, for individuals to act simultaneously in such harmony? If that were true, they contend, revolution would be at best absurd and at worst impossible. Sartre addresses this criticism directly: 'The question is not, and never has been, as some have believed, how separate particles could constitute a totality.'[10] This view presupposes that individuals are discreet atoms who think and act in total isolation. In that case the harmony of thousands or millions of distinct epicentres of social action would indeed be absurd. In history we are faced not with Locke's atomised individual but with with 'an excess of unifications'. Totalisations criss-cross continuously; communities of action emerge and disappear all the time. Networks and commonalities are already constituted and are reconstituted at every moment. 'The important thing, therefore, is to find out how far the multiplicity of individual syntheses can, as such, be the basis for a community of objectives and of actions,'[11] A perfect harmony of totalisations does not exist and is not even contemplated by Sartre, yet human beings do act together all the time, forming partial totalisations which overlap and conflict, but which insert individuals into a common culture none the less. Sartre writes,

> It is also true that there is no synthetic unity of the multiplicity of totalisations, in the sense of a hypersynthesis which would become, in transcendence, a synthesis of syntheses. What actually happens is that the unity of the all *is*, within each actual synthesis of the same group, in so far as it is *also* the interiority of this other synthesis.[12]

The opposition between the projects of an individual and of all humanity is thus a false one that overlooks the true conditions of group praxis.

The group cannot maintain its state of fusion forever. The intensity of the initial formation, which Sartre calls an Apocalypse, gradually disappears. For the group is not a fixed and frozen entity. Born out of common praxis, it must be continually reformed, over and over again. Commitments and objectives must be stated and restated, changing with the exigencies of external and internal events. The group is not, Sartre insists, an inert totality, but a living structure of practices. Far from an organism that rises above its members in some superior reality, the group is the multiplicity of the totalisations of each individual.

The first requirement faced by the fused group, one which initiates its process of transformation, is some degree of permanence. Somehow the group must ensure its survival. Since it has no ontological status, the group can persist only through the commitments of its members. The need for permanence must itself become an objective of the membership. In the example of 1789, the ruling powers continue to pose a threat after the taking of the Bastille. The revolutionary group must form itself into an efficient mechanism of social change. The objective now is not simply the immediate one of attacking the fortress but of preserving the relationships among the spontaneously formed crowd. The need for permanence changes the internal structure of the group:

> Individual *praxis* interiorises the objective permanence of the common danger in the form of a common exigency. But this new state of the group (which manifests itself historically in every revolutionary situation) is defined by new characteristics, conditioned by new circumstances.[13]

Sartre calls the new structure the 'surviving group'. The situation of the surviving group is perilous. The enemy represents an external danger; but there is an internal enemy as well, one that is no less threatening. Since every individual is free, anyone might defect.

The group is exposed to the freedom of its members to leave, to retotalise the situation, to change their projects. The same freedom that was the basis of the group now becomes its mortal enemy. But Sartre insists that it is not really freedom that threatens the group. Instead the danger lies in the return of the practico-inert, of seriality. Not freedom, but the possibility of re-interiorising seriality in some form is the ultimate danger confronting the group. Consequently, the group is pervaded by fear.

The response of the group to the fear that threatens its survival is the pledge. The mechanism of the pledge, as in the Tennis Court Oath of 1789, is designed to prevent members from leaving or defecting. It is an affirmation by each individual of his revolutionary project. Sartre contends that the introduction of the pledge, although it changes the status of the group, does not destroy common praxis. The pledge does not inject seriality into the group. It is a form of alterity but one that does not endanger freedom. Sartre describes the effect of the pledge on the group as follows: 'As soon as the pledge is given, reciprocity becomes *centrifugal*: instead of being a lived, concrete bond, produced by the presence of two men (with or without mediation), it becomes the bond of their absence.'[14] The spontaneous gathering in front of the Bastille is over. The group, made permanent by the pledge, can now disperse for the night assured that tomorrow people will regroup for another battle.

The other side of the pledge, however, is the terror. Along with the fraternity that comes from group experience goes violence, violence against the enemy and violence against group members who turn to the enemy. In the heat of 1789, the revolution committed regicide, but it also guillotined its children. Danton, Robespierre and the long list of executed rebels attest to the violence associated with revolution. Critics of Sartre accuse him of glorifying this violence, of providing it with theoretical legitimacy, just as he celebrated politically the violence of third world liberation movements in Algeria, Vietnam, Cuba, Madagascar and elsewhere. Indeed Sartre associates revolutionary violence with the 'reciprocity of love'.[15]

Like his friend Merleau-Ponty in *Humanism and Terror*

(1947), Sartre acknowledges forthrightly the role of violence in social change, and in all history. But violence, for Sartre, is not an end in itself. It is not a proof of manliness or racial superiority. Nor does Sartre make distinctions between types of violence as do those who justify 'progressive' or 'proletarian' violence. On the contrary, Sartre views violence as a fact, a difficult fact but a fact none the less. Violence is associated with freedom in the struggle against alienation. Sartre maintains that

> Terror is jurisdiction: through the mediation of all, everyone agrees with everyone else that the permanent foundation of every freedom should be the violent negation of necessity, that is to say, that, in everyone, freedom as a common structure is the permanent violence of the individual freedom of alienation.[16]

Paradoxically, the group initiates the terror in the fraternity of human freedom.

The pledge alone does not ensure the survival of the group. In the course of events an internal differentiation takes place with individuals performing separate tasks: 'the group, waiting for the attack, looks for positions to occupy, divides itself so as to man all of them, distributes weapons, assigns patrol duties to some, and scouting or guard duties to others, establishes communications'.[17] The unity of common praxis (taking the Bastille) gives way in part to the specialisation of functions. The group undergoes a further transformation: it becomes an organisation. Sartre defines the new structure: 'The word "organisation" refers both to the internal action by which a group defines its structures and to the group itself as a structured activity in the practical field, either on worked matter or on other groups.'[18] The drama of the new group structure concerns the fate of common praxis: will the unity that gave birth to the group dissolve under the pressure of the division of labour? Can common praxis be preserved as each individual or sub-group goes about its separate task?

Sartre contends that the organisation does not destroy group solidarity. What happens is that a new practice is developed – active passivity – in which individuals pursue the common end indirectly through their particular functions. The division of labour by itself does not introduce alienation, Sartre maintains, even though Marx, in certain places did so argue.[19] The commitment of the individual to his particular function does not undermine his participation in common praxis. Quite the contrary, 'This common undertaking manifests itself in the individual act which actualises function on the basis of concrete circumstances and it is through this act that the undertaking advances to its end.'[20] Sartre argues that seriality need not be the consequence of specialisation. Even groups with a complex division of labour are compatible with freedom.

To convince the reader, Sartre resorts to the unlikely example of a soccer team. 'However else they may differ, a football team and a group of armed rebels have one thing in common, from the present point of view: that the real objectification of the action of each member lies in the movement of common objectification.'[21] Like the revolutionaries, the soccer players have a common end and a differentiation of tasks and these are balanced in such a way that the two enhance each other. To the extent that the goalie can block a difficult kick, he performs his special task but he also contributes to the common end. When the team plays well, the separation of tasks is not rigid: players know each others' strengths and weaknesses and will come to each others' assistance, stepping out of their assigned position as the occasion demands. Unlike a bureaucracy, the division of labour here is subordinated to the common purpose. The aim of each player or rebel is not to cover their responsibilities but to assist in the victory. Although the organisation resembles a bureaucracy in a superficial way, the balance of particular and common ends is different, tipped, in the case of the organisation, in favour of unity. Alterity or otherness has been introduced into the group: the goalie recognises himself as other than the defenceman, as having a different project. Yet the unity of the group overrides the differences, eliminating the alienating effects of alterity: 'the important point is that the group reinteriorise alterity the better to struggle against it'.[22] When a team plays well together, the different functions blend together in a harmony that incarnates the common purpose:

The true work of organisation is the synthetic production and the distribution of tasks, but also that it must constantly effect the synthesis of the mediated reciprocities which arise in different layers of the common reality. The organised group cannot be practical and alive except as a progressive synthesis of a plurality of reciprocal fields.[23]

Sartre here demonstrates against his critics that relations with others are not always alienating. For Sartre the world is not a hostile screen against which the individual loses himself. On the contrary, only with others, in the struggle against scarcity, can individual freedom appear in its fullness.

From the fused group to the organisation, the collective promotes individual freedom. If Sartre writes that individual praxis is the only basis of dialectical intelligibility, so groups are the only foundation of freedom. In the analysis of the group, Sartre's concept of the individual has not prevented or obscured historical comprehension. Although individual praxis is the starting point of Sartre's marxism, it is only the abstraction that makes concrete understanding possible. The concepts of the series and the group constitute the opposite poles of praxis. They and the variations between them are the basic categories of dialectical reason. Individual action is the means to explore them, nothing more. In the historical field, individual action, in fact does not exist. It is always incorporated in series and groups.

From the fused group to the organisation, Sartre had been discussing individual praxis, or, what he calls the constituent dialectic. In each case, it was a question of how individuals acted in common from the perspective of the individuals. At this point he introduces the notion of the constituted dialectic by which he means group action itself. Group action, he writes, 'belongs to every individual *praxis* as an interiorised unity of multiplicity'.[24] The question now is to see if the constituted dialectic is indeed made intelligible by dialectical reason. What are, in other words, the types of being characterised by 'the common action of the organised group *in so far as it is common*'?[25] The *leitmotif* of the discussion continues to be the question of the introduction of the practico-inert. Is the freedom that characterised the fused group and the organisation threatened by the constituted dialectic? Does group action imply necessarily a return to seriality and therefore to alienation?

Sartre argues that common praxis is not of a different order from individual praxis. Group action does not represent a being that stands above the individuals, unintelligible to them. Group action is subject to the same type of analysis as individual action. In both cases, it is a question of the introduction of forms of inertia and the response to them. The group does not act mysteriously by itself according to a different set of laws and operations. It continues to betray the same dialectic of human beings and things that was displayed everywhere else in the *Critique*. The difference is one of degree: group action (the constituted dialectic) makes possible a greater amount of passivity and inertia than individual action in a fused group or organisation.

The example Sartre invokes to differentiate between the constituent and constituted dialectic is the case of disagreements within the group. What happens when one individual or sub-group thinks the group as a whole should follow one course of action and another individual or sub-group favours a different path? The consequence of the disagreement must be that the solution chosen will be common to the group but represent a certain passivity to those whose path was not adopted. The group will be preserved through the common action but only through the introduction of seriality. If, in a given factory, management and workers disagree about a certain job, the solution, normally the position favoured by management, renders the group action other for the workers.

According to Sartre it does not matter if the solution was arrived at by fiat from above or by democratic procedures. Sartre attacks the notion that 'an agreement of minds' can settle disputes better than commands from above. Liberals who advocate consensus theory are misguided, in Sartre's opinion, when they think that a democratic vote settles issues without changing the status of the unity of the group. When a vote is taken some win and some lose. The losers must respond to the common action differently from the winners; they must see it as other. For Sartre, 'what is really involved is a resurrection of unity through seriality and the creation of groups in the serial milieu *without the dissolution of alterity'*.[26] When the unity of sub-groups is based on otherness, the notion of the agreement of minds 'remains abstract and quite inessential'. Attempts to introduce consensus theory into marxism, like Habermas' notion of the public sphere in which free discussion is the basis of socialist transformation, remain flawed. They represent an idealist distortion of group praxis in which intellectual homogeneity is equated with group unity.

Now that group action has been reorganised, after the solution of the disagreement, inertia has become part of the collectivity. As Sartre puts it, 'the constituted dialectic rests on a non-dialectical moment: that of adopted inertia'.[27] This means that while each individual still makes a project of group action, the nature of group action has changed. The individual who was in opposition must interiorise the otherness of the solution in order for group action to continue. Group praxis remains the totalisation of the individuals within it, but it has lost a certain transparency or lucidity. Sartre argues that 'the intelligibility of the constituted dialectic is weighed down and degraded in comparison to the full intelligibility of the constituent dialectic'.[28]

To explain the difference between the two types of praxis Sartre introduces a distinction between praxis and process. Group praxis, burdened by adopted inertia, includes a machine-like element that is absent from the constituent dialectic. Each sub-group responds to the apparatus of the group as if it were other. The whole begins to resemble a machine whose parts are integrated in common action through complete externality. Sartre writes,

> The group tends to have more in common with the kind of complex which is constituted by a machine and by the workers who use it for a particular job than with practical organisms which dialectically transcend every inert moment of the worked object, every organisation of the practical field.[29]

Since the action of a machine can be termed a process, as distinct from a praxis, the dialectical intelligibility of group action must be considered a combination of praxis and process.

Common praxis includes, like individual praxis, 'a common aim, objectification, labour, transcendence, reciprocal adaptation'.[30] What is new in common praxis, however, is passivity and inertia. Action appears to the individual as occurring in some 'elsewhere', a place which he or she cannot identify. Instead of emerging from within him or herself, as from within all other individuals, group action orginates as externality. The group resembles not a tight unity but a multiplicity in unity, a dispersed unity. Nevertheless, the series has not taken over completely. Group action remains praxis. At this point, therefore, process is still different from the atomisation of the series for the simple reason that it can be reversed at any time. Process in fact must be seen as action against seriality: it is the attempt of the group to continue in its unity against the introduction of inertia. The intelligibility of group process, Sartre contends, 'comes from the fact that it can be dissolved and reversed; in fact, it simply represents the moment where the interior action of the group intensifies so as to counteract the multiplicity which begins to erode it'.[31]

Having included process within dialectical reason, Sartre can conclude that group action is fully intelligible. The constituted dialectic no less than the constituent dialectic is subject to the principles of comprehending the mediation of men and things. Group action like individual action preserves the marxist thesis that man makes history:

> Both as object and as subject of the constituted dialectic, the group produces itself in complete intelligibility, since it is possible to see how every determination in inertia transforms itself, in it and through it, into a counter-finality or a counter-structure (and, also, in the best cases, into structures and finality); this intelligibility is dialectical because it shows us the free, creative development of a practice.[32]

Unlike organisational group praxis, the institution represents a return to seriality. Through conflicts and disagreements the institution evolves out of the organisation as common practice recedes farther and farther away from the individual. Sub-groups become more distinct and hierarchy becomes more rigid. For Sartre the institution furnishes the acid test of dialectical reason. Earlier cases of group action posed no difficulty. Indeed Sartre goes so far as to identify the unity of the group with his definition of existence from *Being and Nothingness*. He writes,

> Now this practical, dialectical unity which was the group and which causes it to negate it in its very effort at integration, is simply what we have elsewhere called *existence*. The final problem of intelligibility arises on this basis: what must *a group be in its being in order to negate existence in and of itself* and in order to realise its own common ends in the object as the amplification of ends which have been freely posited by practical organisms as free dialectical existences?[33]

In the institution praxis becomes other. The struggle against seriality in this case results in the erection of pure sovereignty: all unity must be centralised in the battle against external danger and internal treachery. In order for the group to be maintained, alterity must become its principle. In the common action of the institution everyone becomes other. Purges and the terror become the commonplace strategy to the point where no one is exempt. Common bonds are dissolved through fear and suspicion so that those who are alike become different. Sartre illustrates the formation of the institution by the example of the convention of 1792. The girondins, who were socially identical with the jacobins, became the class enemy. Antagonism was resolved by exclusion and homogeneity was produced from above. This homogeneity was won at great cost since no one was secure from being labelled other. Sartre writes, 'Once those who are *the same* again (they vote the same way and are committed to the realisation of the same policies) have become simultaneously and secretly *Others*, alterity becomes the secret truth of unity for everyone.'[34]

For Sartre the institution represents an important reversal in the dialectical process. It is the effort to make the group into the individual. Under the institution the group becomes the subject and the members become its objects. 'The fundamental modification consists in transferring *the common being of the group*, regulatory freedom and impossible ontological unity to the *praxis* of the group as such.'[35] The institution embodies the ontological impossibility of making the group into a subject. Collective freedom becomes incorporated into an inorganic object. It thereby loses its quality as freedom and introduces inertia into the heart of group action. Because the group cannot be a subject (only the individuals in the group are subjects) it becomes an object which must be interiorised by each member. If group action is praxis and process, institutional group action is praxis and thing.

The institution is a scandal to Sartre. Attempting to preserve group unity, it only inaugurates separation, multiplicity and alterity. It is, he says, 'praxis as other'. The institution is an index of the collapse of the group amidst its preservation. The materiality it introduces is twofold: individuals pledge themselves to inertia and they do so in 'serial impotence'. In the institution freedom is 'completely hidden' behind inert unity. A new type of human being is created in the institution, one who resembles a machine. Man in an institution is a 'forged tool'. The individual must make a project of being totally other than himself, of adopting a role prescribed for him and defined from above, from a complete other. He acts as other to others who are other to him. The institution for Sartre is a travesty of the dialectic: 'The institutional moment, in the group, corresponds to what might be called the systematic self-domestication of man by man. The aim is, in effect, to create men who (as common individuals) will define themselves, in their own eyes and amongst themselves, by their fundamental relation (mediated reciprocity) with institutions'.[36] The mediation of human beings and things in this case is the opposite of what it was in the fused group.

In addition to introducing seriality into the group, the institution establishes authority as the guarantor of unity. The institution cannot rely upon the individual's project of group unity because individuals are now partially serialised, separate from one another and engrossed only in their particular functions. The leader must stand in place of common praxis as the sole force opposing reserialisation. The leader 'reinteriorises' the externality that has crept into the group. He becomes the group incarnate, the focal point of a unity that was once dispersed throughout the group. The leader thus holds together two sides of the contradiction that permanently threatens the group's existence: 'they represent both the irresistible force of transcendent *praxis* and the permanent possibility that it will break up into serial relations of seriality'.[37]

Like Marx, Sartre argues against the position that leaders create institutions. On the contrary, the place of the leader is established only in the context of organisations that have become petrified into institutions. Leadership, Sartre writes, 'is itself produced by the inert eternality of institutional relations'.[38] Theories of charismatic authority (Max Weber) or elitist theories (Vilfredo Pareto) come under severe criticism by Sartre's argument. The failure of groups to preserve their unity is the condition under which authority comes to rest with the leader. When Hobbes writes that only a strong leader can guarantee social order he forgets that a social order which requires such a leader has already collapsed, that society has already lost the vital commitment of its members.

In this way Sartre dismisses the problem of legitimacy: there are no legitimate leaders since authority is always based on the coercion necessary to bring partially serialised individuals into conformity with the goals of the group. Force alone can insure that passivised individuals will adhere to the group, rather than disperse into seriality. Although force can take many forms and exist in different degrees, it remains essential to the structure of the institution. A legitimate leader is therefore a contradiction in terms: if individuals voluntarily adhered to the group, the leader would be superfluous; if the leader is supported by the group some degree of force already conditions that response.

With leaders and a hierarchical apparatus, institutions

confront the rest of society. In particular, institutions play an important role in dominating serialised individuals. When an institution comes into contact with non-grouped individuals a new kind of praxis is formed. Sartre completes the discussion of the series, as outlined in the previous chapter, by indicating how the atomised series is subject to the manipulation of the institution. Readers of newspapers and radio audiences are not only subjected to the externality of the practico-inert; they are also actively organised into serial impotence by institutions. Sartre contends that

> what is lived and used as collective by the serial flight of alterity is *also* an organised group (the newspaper) or an institutional group (the state radio) which, in a common undertaking transcends itself towards collectives and inert gatherings as their own objective.[39]

The effects of institutions are not limited to their members but extend to the heart of society itself. Sartre's analysis points to a complex play between institutions and society which has great value for historical materialism. It provides a basis for demonstrating the connection between workers in an institution and the general population. The relation between the institution and serialised individuals is not one of class. Yet a strong bond and common fate connnects the working class with the world of everyday life.

The potential for social control is realised most fully in the state, the institution *par excellence*. In defining the role of the state, Sartre points out that large-scale societies are not groups, but congeries of all types of groups: series, organisations, institutions, even fused groups. The state therefore, cannot be considered, as conservatives would wish, an emanation of the entire society.

> In short, what is known as the State can never be regarded as the product or expression of the totality of social individuals or even of the majority of them, since this majority is serial *anyway*, and could not express its needs and demands without liquidating itself as a series, so as to become a large group.[40]

Instead the state is one institution among many and acts to

manipulate and control other collectives. Like other institutions the state depends on the impotence of seriality to provide an arena for its control.

Sartre agrees with Marx that the state is tied to the ruling class. He sees the state more as a mediation between contending elements within the ruling class than as a simple expression of it. The state is not a mere executive committee of the ruling class. Nor is it an 'epiphenomenal abstraction' determined by the mode of production. For Sartre, the state as an institution is a specific form of praxis with its own effects upon society. In the end, however, Sartre agrees with the general marxist position that the state is doubly determined: it serves the interests of the ruling class and it strives for national continuity. 'The State therefore *exists* for the sake of the dominant class, but as a practical suppression of class conflicts within the national totalisation.'[41]

The strength of Sartre's analysis of the institution rests with his definition of the new form of practice it produces. When an institution acts repeatedly on a series it produces a form of practice in the series which Sartre calls 'other-direction' (*extéreo-conditionnement*), a term borrowed from David Reisman's *The Lonely Crowd* although put to distinctly Sartrean uses. In the context of a series which is defined institutionally through racism, the practice of individuals takes on an extreme degree of alterity.

> To allow this unified milieu [of racism] to exist fully through recurrent dispersal, it is necessary and sufficient that every Other should make himself completely other, that is to say, that he should direct his free *praxis* onto himself so as to be *like the Others*.[42]

A ghetto black is defined by American institutions as undesirable, shiftless, criminal and so forth. That black must make himself into that image; the external otherness must become internal. If the institution were to work perfectly, the black would not even have the resort of fellow blacks. The institution would prevent the emergence of a black community, encouraging instead the continued seriality of blacks. Other-direction differs from seriality in that it represents more than the interiorisation of material passivity. In the case of people waiting for the bus, each individual is actively enrolled, so to speak, in the queue. The bus and driver were simply out there in the social field, available but not insistent. In the case of other-direction, the institution actively seeks out members of the series, designating them as it chooses. Here the serialised individual must interiorise a force that is seeking him out. Other-direction is a more nefarious form of practice than seriality. Sartre's concept of other-direction provides the basis for a compelling critique of contemporary society with its over-abundance of bureaucratic institutions: 'what is apparent today', he writes, 'at this moment of History, in which the structures of other-direction are more manifest in and around us is, in fact, the crucial importance of these structures for the comprehension of historical events'.[43]

Sartre is just as interested in the effects of institutional practice on the leader as he is in the force of other-direction on the series. The inexorable law of institutions is that the leader must gather unto himself more and more power as inertia continues to threaten the group's existence. Sartre explores the dynamics of this tendency in the case of a bureaucracy, a complex, hierarchically-organised institution. The effect of bureaucratic authority is that no one can take charge but the leader. Each bureaucrat is a possible leader to those below and a possible subject to those above. The bureaucrat will deny his power, however, because this would lead to suspicions by those on his own level as well as by his superiors. As a result, a power vacuum is created in which all authority sweeps upwards towards the leader. But even the leader is powerless to animate 'the pyramid of mechanisms' below. Bureaucracy becomes stifled by its own inertia. In this situation, with passivity multiplying itself *ad infinitum*, the cult of personality emerges as the only force that can bring energy back into the system. The ultimate effect of the institution upon the leader therefore is deification.

Sartre discusses bureaucracy and the cult of personality in relationship to the Soviet Union where his analysis has obvious relevance. In fact, the manuscripts for the second volume of the

Critique, which constitute a good-sized book, are concerned predominantly with the case of the Soviet Union.[44] At the time of writing the *Critique*, though he opposed stalinism and even a leninist party, Sartre was unwilling to give up all hope for socialism in Russia. After demonstrating how well stalinism fits with his analysis of bureaucracy, Sartre pulled back. Even though he rejected the dictatorship of the proletariat as an 'absurd' idea, he was unwilling to relegate Soviet socialism to the hell of bureaucratic inertia:

> The internal contradictions of the socialist world bring out, through the immense progress that has been made, the objective exigency for debureaucratisation, decentralisation, and democratisation: and this last term should be taken to mean that the sovereign must gradually abandon its *monopoly of* the group.[45]

With a generous wave of the hand Sartre dismissed the logic of his own argument. According to the *Critique*, the only way to be rid of bureaucracy is revolution; the formation of fused groups which would initiate a new cycle moving from series to groups and groups to series. Instead Sartre resorts to the *deus ex machina* of the enlightened despot, the great bureaucrat who would renounce his power and restore organisational vitality to the rotting institutional corps. Yet the logic had not been outlined by which 'the sovereign' would 'gradually abandon its monopoly' of power.

Sartre's concept of the group, with all its permutations, has been criticised for circularity and therefore for undue pessimism. Critics charge that the movement from the series to the group and back again from the fused group to the institution offers a bleak account of history, one which fails to consider the cumulative progress that has occurred. This criticism could be sustained only if Sartre were in fact writing history. But that is not the case. Sartre's panorama of group formations is not intended as an historical logic, but only as a representation of the possibilities and a confirmation of their dialectical intelligibility. Sartre does not claim that every fused group must lead to an organisation and every organisation to an institution, in the manner of Weber's theory of the routinisation of charisma. What he does try to demonstrate is that within the field of history dialectical reason is capable of comprehending the active role of human beings, even in situations like institutions in which their projects do not emerge transparently.

A stronger case against Sartre's theory of groups can be made on the basis that it fails to attend to societies as a whole, concentrating instead on small groups. Ironically, the theory which places totalisation at the centre of history loses sight, in this argument, of the forest for the trees. The transformation of societies is obscured from view as the Sartrean lens is focused on the microscopic world. Series and groups are categories appropriate to small groups, as Sartre himself admits, not to whole societies. This criticism, potentially very damaging, is addressed in the final section of the *Critique*.

Finally, Sartre's theory of groups contains a flaw similar to one that plagued his theory of individual praxis. He has a tendency to fall out of the mode of social theory into another level of discourse. Individual praxis was reduced, in some places in the text, to moral individualism. In a parallel fashion, the theory of groups becomes at times a moral theory. In the following excerpt taken from the interview, 'Self portrait at seventy', Sartre speculates about social relations in a society beyond scarcity:

> In order for true social harmony to be established, a man must exist entirely for his neighbour, who must exist entirely for him. This cannot be realised today, but I think that it will in the future, once there has been a change in the economic, cultural, and affective relations among men. It will begin with the eradication of material scarcity – which, as I showed in the *Critique of Dialectical Reason*, is for me the root of the antagonisms, past and present, among men.[46]

This passage presages a society of total transparency. Instead of common practice leading to mutual recognition, Sartre imagines a world of moral perfection. Each individual will live 'entirely for his neighbour' as in the Christian maxim. The necessary difference between individuals engaged in free praxis has collapsed into moral homogeneity. Texts such as this encourage critics to argue that

Sartre has not changed since *Being and Nothingness* (1943) and the essay 'Existentialism is a humanism' (1945) where a form of Kantian morality was evident. Fortunately these passages are rare and misleading when taken as a representation of Sartre's position. The strengths of Sartre's theory of groups in the *Critique* cannot be dismissed because of his occasional retreat into moralism in interviews.

The final section of the *Critique* examines the play of all forms of praxis, from series to institution, in the historical field. History itself is still not approached. Sartre remains concerned with the 'formal milieu in which the historical concrete must necessarily occur'.[47] At this level, the mixture of series, collectives, fused groups, organisations and institutions reveals a circle. The line that follows the increasing complexity of social praxis also marks the circularity of the dialectic. As more and more inertia appears within groups, the petrified institution fragments into the series. Both linear and circular, diachronic and synchronic, the dance of human beings and things in complex mediation confirms the intelligibility of dialectical reason.

The value of this intelligibility is tested by a reexamination of the working class, viewed not as a single group praxis but as part of the historical field. In such a light, the working class appears in all its complexity. It is an amalgam of series, fused groups and institutions. Sartre underlines the complexity of the working class as follows:

> The important point for us is that in everyday action, the working class defines its practical unity *as a totalisation* of objective but inert practical significations, issuing from a sovereign who himself exists only in exteriority and as a patient dissolution of serial forces of inertia which are also no more than the class itself *in its being*, in the course of a regroupment which is aimed at a transcendent objective which has to be defined as *Praxis-process*. The working class is neither pure combativity, nor pure passive dispersal nor a pure institutionalised apparatus. It is a complex, moving relation between different practical forms each of which completely recapitulates it, and whose true bond with one another is totalisation.[48]

The complexity of the internal structure of the working class conflicts with the view of the party as well as with that of liberal sociologists. The working class is neither a united revolutionary army nor a complacent, consuming citizenry. Rather it is a complex totality united only in contradiction. Both '*praxis* and inertia, dispersal of alterity and common field'.[49] the working class is comprehensible as a synthetic movement which continually unites these discrete types of praxis.

Given the multiplicity of working class praxis, one can question its unity within a single totalisation. Is it possible for the working class to totalise the entire historical field, as the marxist concept of revolution demands? To answer this question Sartre returns to the beginning of his presentation, to the concept of labour acting against the practico-inert. He argues that the working class can totalise history because the mode of production is its internal dynamic. Sartre's marxism preserves the traditional view of the working class as the bearers of man's fate. In the following passage Sartre integrates the concept of the mode of production into his analysis, presenting the working class not so much as the universal class in Marx's sense, but as the unifiers in the struggle against scarcity:

> if the mode of production is the infrastructure of every society in human history, this is because labour . . . is the infrastructure of the practico-inert (and of the mode of production), not only in the sense of diachronic totalisation . . . but also synchronically since all the contradictions of the practico-inert and especially those of the economic process are necessarily constituted by the constant re-alienation of the worker in his labour, that is to say, by practice in general in this *other world* which it constructs, sacrificing itself so that it can exist. . . . From this viewpoint, if the foundation of the class struggle is to lie in the practico-inert, this is in so far as the objective conflict of interests is both received and produced by passive activity and reveals itself in labour (or in all kinds of behaviour) as a reciprocity of antagonism − possibly in a petrified form and, for example, as an exigency of the tool or machine.[50]

Hence there is a happy ending, with Sartre looking more like a marxist than ever.

Although Sartre rejoins traditional marxism in this passage, it is on his own terms. The mode of production is the social infrastructure and labour is the central category of social analysis. The abstract struggle between human beings and things has become the possibility of the victory of the working class over scarcity. Sartre reminds the marxists that even for Marx the class struggle was part of a larger conflict between man and nature. The ultimate enemy in Marx's terms is the realm of necessity; for Sartre it is the totality of practices which have been constructed within alienation along the path of history. Placed in the heart of these alienated apparatuses, at the point where free praxis confronts inert matter, the working class can play the role of grand synthesiser, scooping up all the mediations within a single totalising bag that mankind will carry through the jungle of history towards the paradise of a new world.

Sartre's reaffirmation of the working class is both exhilarating and disappointing. It is exhilarating in the sense that he has been able to combine his sense of subjectivity with the traditional marxist position. But it is disappointing in the sense that the renewed marxism in this case is not, after all, much different from the old. More specifically, along the path of conceptual elaboration, Sartre stopped at many points to show how dialectical reason contained greater potential for comprehending human alienation than that realised within contemporary marxism. Not only the workplace but the world of everyday life was subjected to scrutiny for signs of alterity, passivity and alienation. The basis was being laid for a more sweeping critical theory than that provided by orthodox marxism. One could anticipate that domination in all forms would become the object of dialectical reason. The plight of women and children in history was thus to be given its due. But such is not the case. Labour and the workplace are reaffirmed as the vortex of historical time and the only form of domination that is included in the final totalisation is that of exploited wage labour.

There were many hints, from the beginning of the *Critique*, that this would be Sartre's conclusion. Most prominently Sartre theorised the first totalisation as that of need. Desire, the dialectical opposite of need, was left out of the account. The logical consequences followed accordingly: need as the first totalisation became the basis of the final totalisation. The working class confronting the mode of production is only a highly intricate elaboration of the individual facing the natural world in search of food. But a dialectic based on desire might lead to different conclusions. It might begin with an individual confronting the world in search of a sexual object and end with a presentation of the complex structures (including the workplace) through which men dominate women. It might also include a discussion of commodity fetishism, not only in Marx's sense as an inversion of relations between human beings and things obscuring the labour process, but also in terms of the act of consumption as an imaginary appropriation of reified signs. By reaffirming the primacy of labour and the mode of production Sartre has missed the chance to transcend the limitations of traditional marxism so as to account for forms of domination that play a significant role in contemporary radical thought.

The totalising synthesis of the working class is not restricted, however, to overcoming the practico-inert. Sartre realises that the struggle against scarcity is played out as a class struggle, as a conflict of group against group rather than as a conflict of human beings against things. The place of the class struggle in the totalisation of history must therefore be taken into account.

Sartre begins the discussion of the class struggle with a critique of analytical reason. Positivism takes the practico-inert determinations and breaks them down into isolated units. Such a procedure distorts the study of class relations by ignoring the role of praxis. Dialectical reason alone is appropriate:

> It is possible to discover something like meaning in the development of societies and men provided we recognise that the reciprocal relations of groups, of classes and generally of all social formations . . . are *basically practical*, that is to say, that they realise themselves through reciprocal activities of mutual aid, alliance, war, oppression, etc.[51]

In the first instance, the class struggle is intelligible as the practical movement against another group, regardless of the apparent passivity of the oppressed:

> Our dialectical investigation shows the double determination of constituted *praxis*. At every level, even inside a group as soon as it ceases to be fused, constituted *praxis* is characterised by lateral flight, that is to say, by various forms of inertia, alterity and recurrence. At the *same time*, and *even in a collective*, constituted *praxis* retains its basic character as a dialectical activity which transforms the practical field by an *intelligible* reorganisation of means for an end which sees the end as an objective determination of the field of future possibilities on the basis of needs, dangers, 'interests', etc., conditioned by previous circumstances as a whole.[52]

Sartre pleads for an analysis of the class struggle which pursues praxis in all its complexity and finds a totalisation however faint its imprint in the pages of history.

After these introductory arguments Sartre goes on to explore the question of the unity of a class. In marxist theory since Lenin class unity is most frequently seen as the work of a vanguard party which, as the political arm of the proletariat, becomes the active subject of history, in Sartre's terms, the synthetic totaliser. The party *represents* the aims of the working class. Through the long history of socialist movements and governments, the ambiguity of the party's pretension has become only too apparent. The party can come to represent little more than itself as a bureaucratic institution as in the second international and in some eurocommunist parties today. The party can also come to represent a form of tyranny over the working class where it sees itself carrying out socialist construction against the direct wishes of the oppressed who have been corrupted by the old regime or by 'trade union consciousness'. In either case the unity of working-class practice has been absorbed by an institution which stands apart from concrete proletarian aspirations.

The pressing need for a critical study of working-class practice leads Sartre to reject the claims of the party in favour of a careful study of the complexity of the class struggle. He discovers first of all that class unity does not reside exclusively within the class itself. 'Thus the class is connected to its transcendent unity through the mediation of the other class. It is *united* outside itself in the suffered freedom of the Other.'[53] Or again, 'their moving, changing, fleeting, ungraspable yet *real* unity comes to them from other classes in so far as each is bound to all the others by a practical reciprocity of either a positive or a negative kind'.[54] Class is not a unified phenomenon. It must be studied from both ends of the struggle, pitting the perspective of one group against that of the other. The action and attitude of the bourgeoisie towards the working class is a central aspect of the practical field in which the working class acts against the bourgeoisie. Class struggle is thus a reciprocal play of complex groups. If that is so, what is the source of the unifying totalisation that synthesises the movement of history?

The class struggle is not simply a battle of contending practices. It is 'a conflict of rationalities', a struggle over how to interpret the struggle, over which methods and epistemologies are to be employed in writing the sign of history. In that conflict the bourgeoisie employs analytical reason and it must do so since analytical reason obscures the contradictions, reducing them to quantifiable differences. The bourgeoisie must deny, Sartre contends, that there is a class struggle in the first place; it must deny that two sets of practices are locked in mortal combat, determining the fate of mankind. 'The bourgeois class', he writes, 'conceals the operation of the dialectic under the atomising rationality of positivism.'[55] The proletariat, on the contrary, has no resort other than the dialectic. It turns to the dialectic, like a plant to the sun, to counter the rationality of the bourgeoisie, to make its own actions intelligible to itself and to further its struggle against the capitalist mode of production. 'We can conclude by saying that the dialectic, as the practical consciousness of an oppressed class struggling against its oppressor, is a reaction which is produced in the oppressed by the divisive tendency of oppression.'[56] Under the burden of the practico-inert, organised and controlled by the bourgeoisie, the proletariat must reinteriorise worked matter and redefine it in relation to its praxis. The machines are not simply efficient devices, standing there inertly at the behest of workers and for their benefit, alleviating toil like a power lawn-mower in a middle-class suburb. Although technological rationality is a major component of bourgeois ideology, the machines, to the workers, must be reinteriorised as part of the system that oppresses them. The workers therefore turn to the dialectic in practice, redefining the machines as part of the system of scarcity.

Sartre's logic moves to the inevitable conclusion: history can only be interpreted through dialectical reason. The working class can act only by resorting to dialectical reason. Hence the totalisation of history — the only way of making history intelligible — is an affair of the working class. Sartre's words are worth reproducing here:

> The conclusion of this investigation is that *the only possible intelligibility* of human relations is dialectical and that this intelligibility, in a concrete history whose true foundation is *scarcity*, can be manifested only as an antagonistic reciprocity. So class struggle as a practice necessarily leads to a dialectical interpretation; and, moreover, in the history of human multiplicities, class struggle is necessarily produced on the basis of historically determined conditions, as the developing realisation of dialectical rationality. Our History is intelligible to us because it is dialectical and it is dialectical because the class struggle produces us as transcending the inertia of the collective towards dialectical combat-groups.[57]

We are back to Marx's 'riddle of history solved', to Hegel's Absolute Spirit knowing itself in and for itself. The question perhaps is which is it, Hegel or Marx?

In the end, history, for Sartre, is a single totalisation. For Marx that *telos* was defined socially: communist society realises man's essence (*Gattungswesen*). For Hegel that *telos* was defined spiritually: consciousness comes to itself as the realisation of Being. For Sartre, it appears that *telos* is defined epistemologically: as the working class turns to dialectical reason, history is unified in a single act of comprehension. We must turn to Sartre's text to clarify what he calls 'the real problem of History'.

> If History really is to be the totalisation of all practical multiplicities and of all their struggles, the complex products of the conflicts and collaborations of these very diverse multiplicities must themselves be intelligible in their synthetic reality, that is to say, they must be comprehensible as the synthetic products of a totalitarian *praxis*. This means that History is intelligible if the different practices which can be found and located at a given moment of the historical temporalisation finally appear as partially totalising and as connected and merged in their very oppositions and diversities by an intelligible totalisation from which there is no appeal.[58]

Unlike Marx and Hegel, Sartre has not reduced the polyvalence and contingency of history to an eschatological turn of the dialectic. In this passage Sartre is not asserting an absolute presence between knowledge and being, a perfect congruence between the real and the rational which captures completely and finally the odyssey of mankind. Ideas do not exhaust reality but only represent it imperfectly. His claim is far less metaphysical.

The rational value of the single totalisation, the 'one truth', is first, conditional. *If* we are to comprehend history as the struggle against scarcity, *then* the proletariat's dialectical reason is the only resort that enables the process to be made intelligible as a whole. Cast in the conditional mode, dialectical truth is subject to a choice – dare we say, an existential choice – which itself has no ontological privilege. The fact is, as always with Sartre, one must choose: analytical reason leads to the perspective of the bourgeoisie, with all its limitations; dialectical reason leads to the perspective of the proletariat, with the possibility of totalising history. So Sartre has not fallen into metaphysics; he has not been caught in the net of logocentrism because he does not use logic as an anvil to hammer down the multiplicity of history into a single, curtailed reality. In Nietzsche's terms he has not made truth the disguise of his will. His error, as I stated above, rests not with logo-centrism but with restricting the resort of dialectical reason to the proletariat, rather than exploring its play within all oppressed groups.

The conditional mode is strengthened by Sartre's recognition that today there is no totaliser and there may never be one. As he sees it the problem is precisely that: the working class has not turned to dialectical reason, even though it is available to them alone. The problem to be confronted in the second volume of the *Critique* where the actual movement of historical totalisation is to be described and traced is precisely that of a 'totalisation without a totaliser'. Sartre has not closed off the circle, tying dialectical reason with the working class into a metaphysical knot. All the difficulties do not vanish once dialectical reason is accorded its due. The trials of historical practice do not disappear in his text with a flourish of harmonious resolution. Everything remains to be done; the difficult work of discovering the value of dialectical reason in empirical history and the ideological labour of making that knowledge effective in the world.

In the limited terms in which he has defined his project the *Critique* if not totally successful achieves much of its purposes. The formal conditions for historical materialism are presented. The categories of the *Critique* enable marxism to recover the complex play of subject and object, human beings and things, reason and history. Epistemologically the *Critique* raises the heuristic value of the dialectic, demonstrating that its link with the working class need not result in dogmatism and orthodoxy. The critique of the dialectic preserves the dialectic as a critical tool.

5. Conclusions

Sartre's *Critique* is not a work of speculative philosophy in the manner of *Being and Nothingness*. It has the philosophical purpose of demonstrating the intelligibility of history through dialectical reason. Its main accomplishment, however, is theoretical: to provide categories for historical materialism that will restore the subjective side to the story in which man makes history. The main test, then, of the *Critique* must come in empirical studies. The chief categories of the *Critique*, from series and collective to fused group and institution, must prove their worth in the concrete. For some time marxist historians have moved in the general direction outlined by the *Critique*, albeit without reference to Sartre's work or use of his categories. Most notably E. P. Thompson's *The Making of the English Working Class* (1963) and more recently Herbert Gutman's *The Black Family in Slavery and Freedom: 1750–1925* (1976) depict oppressed groups, English artisans and Southern blacks respectively, responding actively to the pressures of the practico-inert. In the face of a hostile, humiliating social system, the blacks are able to form distinctive cultural and community ties through the mechanism of family relations. These cases illustrate well Sartre's notion of group praxis and present convincing examples of the intelligibility of praxis.

Much more work needs to be done along these lines, but the heuristic value of the *Critique* seems certain. Sartre's marxism discourages the mechanical application of the concept of the mode of production and promises to rescue historical materialism from positivism and objectivism. The use of the categories of the *Critique* brings the celestial laws of the dialectic down to earth where the action of men and women, struggling against domination, appears in humane form. Sartre's answer to official marxism is, then, to restore historical materialism as a vital tool of research and understanding. The history of class struggles is demystified, displaced from the formulas of *diamat* where it only justifies the policies of the Soviet Union and communist parties in general. Marxism becomes a device for learning, for new knowledge. Once again there can be surprises which upset the conventional wisdom of the left.

Sartre's marxism does not speak to all the questions that trouble marxists today. There are limits to Sartre's accomplishments which detract from the value of the *Critique*. Historical materialism suffers from weaknesses which Sartre does not address.

The displacement of socialist revolutions from the core to periphery since 1917 calls into quesion the role of the industrial working class. The *Critique* improves on the concept class consciousness/false consciousness, indicating how consciousness/praxis changes in the process of revolution, and how consciousness/praxis is intelligible even when the situation is not revolutionary. What is missing in this account, however, is a discussion of the changes in advanced society that function to obscure class consciousness, in particular the changes in ideology. The work of Antonio Gramsci, the Frankfurt school and Louis Althusser all address this problem. In one way or another, these neo-marxists attempt to develop categories not found in Marx himself which can illuminate the workings of ideology. Sartre's remarks in the *Critique* on this topic are weak,[1] a severe deficiency of the book. Ideology can be explored at the level of institutional practices (Althusser), as a problem of the ideas and structure of intellectuals (Gramsci), as a psychological problem at the level of socialisation (Fromm, Adorno, Reich), or even at the intellectual level. In each case the concern is to place an element of the social formation within politics, to discern how social institutions function to thwart the class struggle. Without an adequate concept of ideology, one must resort, in explaining false consciousness, either to crude materialism which dismisses the problem as idealist and attributes a false homogeneity to the proletariat, or to the findings of bourgeois sociology which

113

view the working class as integrated into capitalism. In other words, it is not enough that Sartre shows how revolutionary consciousness comes about in the most adverse circumstances; marxists must be able to explain why that consciousness is seldom dominant in the twentieth-century European working class.

Similarly, as I have argued above, to become a general radical theory, marxism must, in the context of the twentieth century, develop categories that explore forms of domination outside the workplace. The realm of politics has long been recognised as a weak spot of marxist writing. But other areas, particularly the family, demand attention. Nineteenth-century marxism, which remained tied in many ways to Victorian bourgeois attitudes, did not help. Normally, when faced with a question like the family, marxists respond by proving again the power of the mode of production. They show reassuringly that the mode of production determines everything. In the *Critique* Sartre raised the problem of mediations in response to vulgar materialists. But he did not present the problem properly as one where new theories must be developed to supplement traditional marxism. It is not enough, for example, to affirm the relative autonomy of the family: one must elaborate a theory of the family in which modes of domination particular to it are illuminated.[2]

Another difficult area that Sartre leaves in ambiguity is the problem of the future. Is the socialist revolution to take the form of earlier upheavals or will its course be different? Sartre hints at an answer to this question in an interview:

> The coming revolution will be very different from the previous ones. It will last much longer and will be much harsher, much more profound. I am not thinking only of France; today I identify myself with the revolutionary battles being fought throughout the world. That is why the situation in France, all choked up as it is now, does not drive me to greater pessimism. I can only say that at least fifty years of struggle will be necessary for the partial victory of the people's power over bourgeois power. There will be advances and retreats, limited successes and reversible defeats, in order finally to bring into existence a new society in which all the powers have been

done away with because each individual has full possession of himself. Revolution is not a single moment in which one power overthrows another; it is a long movement in which power is dismantled. Nothing can guarantee success for us, nor can anything rationally convince us that failure is inevitable. But the alternatives really are socialism or barbarism.[3]

Sartre does not foresee a fused group rising to overthrow capitalism in one great Apocalypse, as one might expect after reading the *Critique*. The class struggle will go on, inconclusively for years, with several fused groups forming and dissolving into seriality. And then, one never knows: it might not happen, barbarism is a distinct possibility.

A repeated charge against the *Critique* concerns its alleged pessimism: everything for Sartre is circular, leading from one cycle to the next – nowhere. I have dismissed this accusation in earlier chapters because it forgets the theoretical limits of the *Critique*, which is not at all a work of history. It is worth noting that in the same interview Sartre explicitly rejects the charge of pessimism. In response to Gramsci's words, 'we must fight with pessimism of the mind and optimism of the will', Sartre says, 'If I were convinced that my fight for freedom was necessarily doomed to failure, there would be no sense in fighting. No, if I am not completely pessimistic, it is primarily because I sense in myself certain needs which are not only mine but the needs of every man.'[4] Over and over again in essays and interviews since the *Critique* Sartre has argued for the possibility of struggle. In fact, since 1960, whatever one may think of the success of his politics, he has been in the forefront of all the major battles. The Algerian and Vietnam Wars, the events of May 1968, the defence of maoists in the 1970s – in each case Sartre aligned himself with the progressive forces, in many instances against the Communist Party and in others acting before them. The conclusion to be drawn from the *Critique* is not pessimism. It is perhaps a touch of awe at all the work that remains to be done. In the *Critique* Sartre maintains consistently that a new social order is possible which is beyond capitalism, indeed beyond all forms of scarcity.[5]

Since the appearance of the *Critique* in 1960 Sartre has moved towards the independent marxist position that was implied in the *Critique* itself. From the early 1960s he drifted farther and farther away from the French Communist Party, taking more radical positions than it on both domestic and international issues. During the 1960s, however, he remained a staunch defender of the Soviet Union. His trips there convinced him of the basic success of the first socialist experiment. Sartre's break with the Soviet Union did not come until the invasion of Czechoslovakia in August of 1968. The rumbling of Soviet tanks in Prague shattered for the last time Sartre's belief that Russia could change in a democratic direction. The radically democratic position of the *Critique* finally took hold and from 1968 Sartre consistently advocated an 'anti-hierarchical and libertarian form of socialism'.[6] For the past decade Sartre has displayed a strong suspicion about all institutional forms of marxism. As the *Critique* dictates, the mass party and the leninist party are institutions which alienate and manipulate popular forces.

As one would expect, the events of May–June 1968 in France were the fulcrum of Sartre's recent politics, providing him with an orientation for a new line of radical action. At that time a student protest at the Sorbonne led to the largest strike in the history of France. About ten million workers were out and their protest was independent of the communist trade unions and the Communist Party. The May events were the most severe test of an advanced capitalist society. Capitalism and bureaucracy were challenged as never before. In those weeks of rebellion it appeared that a new left was in formation, one that rejected the traditional revolutionary models of jacobinism and leninism. Like everyone else Sartre was unprepared for what happened yet he quickly came out in support of the students and workers. For May 1968 demonstrated in the streets what Sartre had been saying in the *Critique*: that a revolt against advanced capitalism was possible and that it could take the form of a movement for direct democracy.

The politics of the *Critique* were that of a new left. They were inspired by marxism but when necessary they took issue with self-proclaimed marxist institutions and societies. They spoke to a new situation, that of advanced capitalism, and they aimed at undoing all those institutions which alienated, exploited and reified human beings. At stake was not only the capitalist mode of production but representative democracy, the patriarchal family, the bureaucratic, educational and communications systems. The new left position led Sartre to support the struggles not only of the traditional proletariat but also the popular movements of regionalism, feminism, gay liberation and the guest workers from Algeria. The *Critique* led Sartre to look beyond the workplace for instances of oppression and for radical protests. The new marxism located alienation in the series, in everyday life and that is where Sartre's politics since 1960 found its causes and its issues.

In pursuit of the new politics Sartre explored new avenues of political expression. Unlike classical intellectuals, Sartre came out of his study, went down into the streets to be with the people. In May 1968 he visited the student controlled areas. In the early 1970s he became titular head of a maoist newspaper, *La Cause du Peuple*, because only his name could save it from government repression. When it became necessary, he went into the street to sell copies of it. Although he gave his support to the maoists, he never fully adhered to that movement. Attracted to the cultural revolution in China as an example of a radically democratic politics and sympathetic to the followers of Mao in France, Sartre still held his distance. Unlike other intellectuals who moved from adulating the Soviet Union to idealising communist China, Sartre viewed the new trend with some restraint. The basis of his reservations about China are not completely clear. It is possible that he did not want to make again the mistake he made about the Soviet Union. Or he may have thought that radical politics in Europe are not served by adhering slavishly to the government of China where social conditions were very different.

In addition to participating in May 1968 and in *La Cause du Peuple*, Sartre sought expression for his new politics in television. The government television service offered Sartre the opportunity to present his views to a mass audience in a series of taped interviews.

Although the shows never came about due to a complex set of differences concerning control of the material, Sartre's willingness to participate in television is another example of his effort to alter the traditional limits of the role of the intellectual.

In line with his new political position, Sartre's writings since the *Critique* concerned predominantly political and social questions. He wrote no literature and only a few essays on literary topics. Three books in the 1970s were focused on political questions. In 1974 *On a Raison de se Révolter* appeared. It was the text of discussions Sartre had between 1972 and 1974 with two young radicals, Philippe Gavi and Pierre Victor. What is noteworthy in *On a Raison de se Révolter* is the degree to which Sartre is not the star in these dialogues, but an equal partner in the effort to comprehend recent political issues. In 1976 *Situations X* was published. Four of its seven essays were on political topics; the remaining three were interviews and much of these were devoted to political questions. In 1977 *Sartre par Lui-Même* appeared and once again, although autobiographical in form, the text was heavily concerned with politics. *Sartre par Lui-Même* was a transcript of a film put together from the interviews done for the abortive television programme. In these three books, it is the *Critique* that provides the theoretical framework for the analysis of politics.

After the *Critique* Sartre's major work was *L'Idiot de la Famille*, a long three-volume study of Gustave Flaubert, the nineteenth-century French novelist. Like the *Critique*, *L'Idiot de la Famille* remains unfinished, with a promised fourth volume that has not appeared. Sartre considers his work on Flaubert to be an application of the concepts of the *Critique*.[7] In that sense all of his writings since 1960 derive from the *Critique*, underscoring its importance in his career. But an argument can be made that the manuscript of the second volume of the *Critique* is a better illustration of the concepts of the *Critique* than *L'Idiot de la Famille*.

L'Idiot de la Famille bears a striking resemblance to two earlier works by Sartre: *Baudelaire* (1946) and *Saint Genet: Comédien et Martyr* (1952). Like the two earlier books, *The Family*

Idiot is an existential psychoanalysis of a great literary figure. The idea of existential psychoanalysis was elaborated in *Being and Nothingness*. In opposition to Freud, whom Sartre considered a determinist, existential psychoanalysis understood the individual on the basis of an original choice of being. In making one's life, each individual chose a special project particular to him which was the basis of his or her entire life. Thus in the case of Genet, the orphan who was caught stealing by his foster parents, to be a thief was the original choice of being. Genet incorporated from the other, his foster parent, a determination of his being as that of a thief. With great subtlety Sartre explored this theme in all of Genet's activities, including his writings.

The same method of existential psychoanalysis is applied in *The Family Idiot* to Flaubert. The main argument that Sartre makes for his method is that it reveals the basic freedom of the individual to choose himself. By the early 1970s, when *The Family Idiot* began to appear, Sartre was placing greater emphasis on the role of history and society in the individual's destiny than he had earlier in *Saint Genet*. In the case of Flaubert Sartre utilises the formidable apparatus of the *Critique* in revealing how Flaubert's original choice of being was at the same time a totalisation of contemporary French society.[8] By internalising his family situation Flaubert makes a choice of himself in such a way that he deals with bourgeois society in general. The basic categories of the *Critique* are in fact employed by Sartre to illuminate Flaubert's life. The individual's project incorporates the totality through numerous complex mediations. The dialectic of individual decision reveals the play of subjective and objective forces. *The Family Idiot* does display the heuristic powers of Sartre's marxism. Yet the choice by Sartre of subject matter is less than ideal. One can properly make the objection that the radical social theory of the *Critique* would have been served better had Sartre completed his analysis of the Soviet Union and its history in volume two than by concentrating on Flaubert. As a testament to the theory enunciated in the *Critique*, *The Family Idiot* is less convincing than a detailed exploration of Soviet history would have been. Sartre's choice of Flaubert reveals a residual adherence to his past as a classical intellectual for whom the comprehension of a great literary figure takes precedence over the story of a revolution. The ambiguity of divided loyalties to the classical intellectual versus the leftist intellectual remains with Sartre to the end.

References

Introduction / pp.9—16

1. Interview with Michel Rybalka in May 1975, forthcoming in the Sartre volume of the Library of Living Philosophers; see also *Sartre by Himself* (trans. Richard Seaver), New York, Urizen 1978, where Sartre expressed his recent opinions on marxism.

2. See 'A friend of the people', and 'A plea for intellectuals', in *Between Existentialism and Marxism* (trans. John Matthews), London, New Left Books 1974, and *On a Raison de se Révolter*, Paris, Gallimard 1974.

3. Cited in Michel-Antoine Burnier, *Choice of Action* (trans. Bernard Murchland), New York, Random House 1968, pp.80—81.

4. These issues are addressed in Mark Poster, *Existential Marxism in Postwar France: From Sartre to Althusser*, Princeton, N.J., Princeton University Press 1975.

1. Reason and Revolution / pp.17—31

1. *Search For a Method* (trans. Hazel Barnes), New York, Vintage 1963, p.xxxiv.

2. ibid. p.7.

3. Sartre does state in passing that new philosophies emerge in 'well-defined circumstances' but he never provides an analysis of these circumstances. He does not show how Descartes/Locke represents one class and Kant/Hegel another.

4. See Louis Althusser, 'Reply to John Lewis' in *Essays in Self Criticism*, London, New Left Books 1976, and *For Marx* (trans. Ben Brewster), London, Allen Lane 1969.

5. *Search For a Method*, op. cit., pp.21—22.

6. Frederick Engels, *Dialectics of Nature* (trans. J. B. S. Haldane), New York, International Publishers 1940.

7. *Search For a Method*, op. cit., p.96.

8. ibid. p.10.

9. ibid. p.97.

10. ibid.

11. ibid. p.99.

12. Herbert Marcuse, *One-Dimensional Man*, London, Routledge and Kegan Paul 1964.

13. *Search For a Method*, op. cit., p.154.

14. ibid. p.56.

15. ibid. p.62; see also Mark Poster, *Critical Theory of the Family*, London, Pluto 1978.

16. *Search For a Method*, op. cit., p.62.

17. Maurice Merleau-Ponty, *Sense and Non-Sense* (trans. Hubert and Patricia Dreyfus), Evanston, Il., Northwestern University Press 1964.

18. *Search For a Method*, op. cit., p.89.

19. ibid. p.90; all italics in quotations are from the original text.

2. The Limits of Dialectical Reason / pp.32–48

1. *Critique de la Raison Dialectique, Précédé de Question de Methode, I. Théorie des Ensembles Pratiques*, Paris, Gallimard 1960; trans. by Alan Sheridan-Smith, London, New Left Books 1976; hereafter cited as *Critique*. There are several commentaries on the *Critique* worthy of mention: Fredric Jameson, *Marxism and Form*, Princeton, N.J., Princeton University Press 1972; R. D. Laing and D. G. Cooper, *Reason and Violence: A Decade of Sartre's Philosophy: 1950–1960*, London, Tavistock 1971; Wilfred Desan, *The Marxism of J. P. Sartre*, New York, Doubleday 1965; and Mark Poster, *Existential Marxism*, Princeton, N.J., Princeton University Press 1976. See also the criticisms by Pietro Chiodi, *Sartre and Marxism* (trans. Kate Soper), London, Harvester Press 1976; Raymond Aron, *History and the Dialectic of Violence* (trans. Barry Cooper), Oxford, Basil Blackwell 1975; and Ronald Aronson, *J.-P. Sartre, The Politics of the Imagination*, London, New Left Books 1978.

2. *Critique*, p.19.

3. ibid. p.23.

4. ibid. p.19.

5. ibid. p.20.

6. ibid.

7. Aron, op. cit.

8. *Critique*, p.43.

9. ibid. p.33.

10. ibid. p.40.

11. ibid. p.50.

12. ibid. p.47.

13. ibid. p.48.

14. For Althusser's attack on the *Critique* see 'Reply to John Lewis' in *Essays in Self Criticism*, London, New Left Books 1976; and for his position on Marx's epistemology see *Reading Capital* (trans. Ben Brewster), London, Allen Lane 1970. The best book on Althusser is Alex Callinicos, *Althusser's Marxism*, London, Pluto 1976.

15. *Critique*, p.66.

16. ibid. p.36.

17. ibid. p.76.

18. ibid. p.40.

19. ibid. pp.56–57.

20. ibid. p.56.

21. ibid. p.52.

22. ibid. p.70.

23. Aron, op. cit., p.21.

24. *Critique*, p.677.

25. To my knowledge Derrida has never addressed himself directly to the *Critique*. Dominick LaCapra, in *A Preface to Sartre*, London, Methuen 1979, offers a Derridean interpretation of Sartre but also does not seriously address the *Critique*.

26. Jacques Derrida, *Of Grammatology* (trans. Gayatri Spivak), Baltimore and London, Johns Hopkins University Press 1976, pp.4–26.

27. *Critique*, p.39.

28. ibid.

29. ibid. p.69.

3. 'Men and Things' / pp.49–80

1. *Critique*, p.79.

2. Karl Marx, 'Theses on Feuerbach', thesis 1, in *Early Writings*, Harmondsworth, Penguin 1975, pp.421–422.

3. *Critique*, p.83.

4. ibid. p.178.

5. ibid. p.123.

6. George Lichtheim, 'Sartre, marxism and history', *History and Theory*, vol. 3 no. 2 (1963), pp.233 ff.

7. Karl Marx, *Capital*, vol. 3, chapter 48, Moscow and London, Lawrence and Wishart 1962, pp.799–800; see also *Karl Marx: Selected Writings in Sociology and Social Philosophy* (ed. T. B. Bottomore and M. Rubel), Harmondsworth, Penguin 1969, pp.259–260.

8. *Critique*, p.125.

9. ibid. p.123.

10. ibid. p.130.

11. ibid. p.134.

12. ibid. p.113.

13. ibid. p.161.

14. ibid. p.151.

15. ibid. p.153.

16. ibid. pp.164–165.

17. ibid. p.172.

18. ibid. p.180.

19. Chiodi, *Sartre and Marxism*, London, Harvester Press 1976, p.24.

20. *Critique*, pp.226–227.

21. Marx, 'A contribution to the critique of Hegel's philosophy of right. Introduction', in *Early Writings*, op. cit., pp.256–257.

22. *Critique*, p.219.

23. ibid. p.208.

24. ibid. p.219.

25. ibid. p.216.

26. ibid. p.210.

27. ibid. p.211.

28. ibid. pp.285–286.

29. ibid. p.221.

30. ibid. p.262.

31. ibid. p.263.

32. ibid. p.286.

33. Georges Lefebvre, *The Great Fear* (trans. Joan White), London, New Left Books 1973.

34. ibid. p.210.

35. *Critique*, pp.297–298.

36. ibid. p.300.

37. ibid. pp.250–251.

38. ibid. p.312.

39. ibid. p.311.

40. ibid. p.316.

41. ibid. p.326.

42. The underlying question is that of the concept of needs. See Agnes Heller, *The Theory of Need in Marx*, London, Allison and Busby 1976.

43. *Critique*, p.107.

44. Sartre's discussion of the concept of structure in the work of Claude Lévi-Strauss (*Critique*, pp.479 ff) does not overcome these difficulties.

45. Marx, *Capital*, vol. 1, chapter 14, section 1, Harmondsworth, Penguin/New Left Review 1976, pp.455–458.

46. *Critique*, p.322.

47. ibid. p.80.

48. ibid. p.220.

4. Groups, Organisations and Institutions / pp.81–111

1. *Critique*, p.354.

2. ibid. p.358.

3. ibid. p.361.

4. ibid. p.364.

5. ibid. p.672.

6. ibid. p.386.

7. ibid. p.387.

8. ibid. p.376.

9. ibid. p.401.

10. ibid. p.391.

11. ibid.

12. ibid. p.400.

13. ibid. pp.412–413.

14. ibid. p.470.

15. ibid. p.439.

16. ibid. p.441. In the same vein, on p.736, Sartre writes, 'the only conceivable violence is that of freedom against freedom through the mediation of inorganic matter'.

17. ibid. p.414.

18. ibid. p.446.

19. Marx, *The German Ideology*, part 1, London, Lawrence and Wishart 1970, pp.50–52.

20. *Critique*, p.459.

21. ibid. p.456.

22. ibid. p.464.

23. ibid. p.479.

24. ibid. p.506.

25. ibid.

26. ibid. p.531.

27. ibid. p.536.

28. ibid. p.539.

29. ibid. p.546.

30. ibid. p.547.

31. ibid. p.552.

32. ibid. p.558.

33. ibid. p.563.

34. ibid. p.593.

35. ibid. p.599.

36. ibid. p.606.

37. ibid. p.618.

38. ibid. p.609.

39. ibid. p.631.

40. ibid. pp.635–636.

41. ibid. p.639.

42. ibid. p.643.

43. ibid. p.652.

44. Publication of these manuscripts is imminent. A partial translation has appeared as 'Socialism in one country', *New Left Review* 100 (November 1976–January 1977), pp.138–163.

45. *Critique*, p.661.

46. 'Autoportrait à soixante-dix ans', in *Situations*, *X*, Paris, Gallimard 1976, p.144. This volume of *Situations* has been translated as *Life/Situations* (trans. Paul Auster and Lydia Davis), New York, Pantheon 1977.

47. *Critique*, p.671.

48. ibid. p.690.

49. ibid. p.701.

50. ibid. p.713.

51. ibid. p.788.
52. ibid. pp.788–789.
53. ibid. p.795.
54. ibid. p.794.
55. ibid. p.802.
56. ibid. p.803.
57. ibid. p.805.
58. ibid. p.817.

5. **Conclusions** / pp.112–120

1. See, *Critique*, p.500.
2. See Mark Poster, *Critical Theory of the Family*, London, Pluto 1978.
3. 'Self-portrait at seventy', *Life/Situations*, New York, Pantheon 1977, p.84.
4. ibid. p.83.
5. *Critique*, p.736.
6. See *On a Raison de se Révolter*, Paris, Gallimard 1974.
7. ibid. p.77.
8. See volume three of *L'Idiot de la Famille*, Paris, Gallimard 1972.

Index

Adorno,T., 45,113
Algeria, 10,14,31,88,115,117
Alienation:
  and dialectical reason, 105; and
  history, 46; and matter, 58–62;
  in Sartre, Hegel and Marx, 62–65;
  and violence, 89; see also Practico-
  inert, Reification
Alterity:
  dispersal of, 104; and groups, 81,93,95,
  96,107; and interest, 66; and pledge,
  88; and series, 76; and working class,
  73
Althusser,L., 15,17:
  and ideology, 113; and marxist
  epistemology, 38–39; and mode of
  production, 77
Analytic reason, 27–28:
  and bourgeoisie, 108,110; and
  dialectical reason, 33–34; and
  objectivity, 78; see also Positivism,
  Sociology and Sociologists
Anti-dialectic, 59,63
Anti-imperialism, 10; see also Algeria,
  Vietnam
Anti-physis, 60
Apocalypse, 87,115
Authority, 96–97

Baran,P., 20
Bastille, storming of, 81–82
de Beauvoir,S., 11
Bloch,E., 15,20
Bourgeoisie, 108–109; see also Ruling
  Class
Bureaucracy, 100

Castoriadis,C., 20
Capitalism, 53,61–64,76–77,117
La Cause du Peuple, 117
Charisma, 97,102
China:
  deforestation of, 59–60; Sartre's
  attitude to, 117
Chiodi,P., 61–63
Classical economics, 54–55
Class:
  consciousness, 24–25,41–43,74–75,
  113; interest, 64–66; position, 41;
  and series, 72–74; struggle, 12,74–75,
  104–105,106–109
Cold war, 10
Commodity fetishism, 53,67,106
Communism, 46,57,62,109
Communist Party, French, 10,11,14:
  Sartre's relationship to, 9,13,115–116
Competition, 68
Comprehension (Verstehen), 40
Convention, of 1792, 95
Consensus, 92–93
Counter-finality, 59
Creativity, 20,28
Croce,B., 46
Cuba, 88
Czechoslovakia, invasion of, 116

Derrida,J., 45–47:
  Of Grammatology, 47
Danton,G., 88
Descartes,R., and cartesianism, 17,51
Depression, of 1929, 76
Desire, 105–106
Determinism, 21,28,83; see also

Freedom, Materialism, Necessity
Dialectic, and dialectical reason:
  constituent and constituted, 91–92,93;
  critique of, 32–48; laws of, 38; and
  objective systems, 78; and scarcity,
  53; subject-object, 50–51,77; see also
  Epistemology, Materialism,
  Proletariat, Totalisation
Dilthey,W., 40
Division of labour, 89–90
Domination, forms of, 55–56; see also
  Family, Women

Engels,F.:
  Dialectics of Nature, 35; see also
  Marx, Nature
Epistemology:
  and dialectical reason, 34–35; and
  individual experience, 44; marxist,
  32–33,38–39; reflection theory, 25
Exteriority see Interiority
Existentialism:
  existential psychoanalysis, 119; and
  marxism, 14,22; and Sartre's social
  theory, 77; see also Merleau-Ponty
Exploitation, 54

False consciousness, 41–43,72,113
Family, 26,114,117
Feudalism, 76
Flaubert,G., 47,118–120
Force, 97; see also Violence
Foucault,M., 39
France:
  cultural life, 20; fourth republic, 13;
  French revolution, 81–82;
  May–June 1968, 115,116–117;
  war-time resistance, 9; see also
  Communist Party, French
Frankfurt School, 15,20,45,113
Freedom:
  and class consciousness, 43; and
  collective, 91; and determinism,
  83–84; and division of labour, 90;
  and fused group, 85–86; in history, 30;

individual, 14; and institution, 96;
  and interest, 65; logic of, 48; and
  necessity, 55,62; and practico-inert,
  74; and violence, 88–89; and working
  class, 13; see also Sartre, *Being and
  Nothingness*
Freud,S., 119
Fromm,E., 113
Future, perspective of, 21,28–29

Genet,J., 119
Girondins, 27,95
Goldmann,L., *Le Dieu Caché*, 20
Grammatology, 46–47
Gramsci,A., 15,113,115
Great Fear, 71–72
Groups, 81–111; and action, 91–94;
  and disagreements, 92–93; fused,
  82–83; and institution, 96–97;
  Sartre's theory of, 101–103; see also
  Instituion, Organisation, Practico-
  inert, Series
Guerin,D., 20
Gutmann,H., *The Black Family in
  Slavery and Freedom*, 112

Habermas,J., 93
Hegel, and hegelianism, 17; and
  Absolute Knowledge, 45; idealist
  dialectic of, 32; on master-slave
  relation, 57–58; *Phenomenology of
  Spirit*, 57; teleology of, 46,50,109;
  see also Alienation, Philosophy
Hierarchy, 95,97–98
History:
  and dialectical reason, 36; and
  logocentrism, 45–46; and marxists,
  34; and praxis, 103–111; telos of,
  28–30,109–110
Hobbes, and hobbesianism, 55,58,97
Horkheimer,M., 45
Human nature, 45
Humanism, Sartre's, 38–39
Hungary, invasion of, 10, 13, 14, 20

Idealism, 50, 51; see also Hegel and hegelianism
Ideology, 44,109,113; see also False consciousness
Individual:
and historical dialectic, 79–80; and institution, 96, 98; Sartre's concept of, 42–45,119; and institution, 96,98; see also Freedom, Groups, Praxis, Sartre, *Being and Nothingness*, Series
Inertia, 58,103,104,107
Institution, 77,94–102
Intellection, 40,46
Intellectuals, 11,113
Interests:
economic, 27; and consciousness, 41–42; see also Alterity, Class
Interiority, and exteriority, 43, 67–68
Intentionality, 40; see also Praxis

Jacobins, and Jacobinism, 27,95,116

Kant, and kantianism, 17,34,38:
Critique of Pure Reason, 34; see also Analytic reason, Dilthey
Kinship, 77
Korean war, 12

Labour:
and alienation, 63–64; and need, 52–53, 55; and practico-inert, 104; primacy of, 106; and social analysis, 105; see also Proletariat
Language, 77
Larzac, 10
Lateral flight, 107
Leader, 97–98,100
Lefebvre,G.:
on 'great fear', 71–72; *Paysans du Nord*, 19–20
Legitimacy, 97
Lenin, and leninism, 38,107,116
Liberals, and liberalism:
and freedom, 70; and humanism, 39; and individual, 44–45; and integration

of working class, 24; and scarcity, 54; see also Consensus, Girondins, Sociology
Literature, 11; see also Flaubert
Locke,J., 17,86
Logocentrism, 45–46, 110
Lukacs,G., 15, 53:
History and Class Consciousness, 50–51; see also Subject

Machines, 65,67,109; see also Technology
Madagascar, 88
Marcuse,H., 20,23–24,45
Market, 54,70
Marx,K., 17:
Capital, 78; and Engels, on scarcity, 54–55; and subject-object dialectic, 53; teleology of, 46,109; 'Theses on Feuerbach', 50; *1844 Manuscripts*, 63; see also Alienation
Marxism:
official, 113; structuralist, 39; traditional, 105; 'Western', 15–16; see also Alienation, Epistemology, Marx, Materialism, Proletariat, Stalinism
Materialism:
dialectical and historical, 35–36; marxist, 33; mechanical, 19,50,113; and scarcity, 54–55; see also Epistemology
Matter, worked, 58–60,68,75–76,82–83
Mediations:
and progressive-regressive method, 24–26;and stalinism, 30
Merleau-Ponty,M:
Adventures of the Dialectic, 12–13; and determinism, 28; *Humanism and Terror*, 12,88; and marxism, 11–13; *Sense and Non-Sense*, 112; *Signs*, 12
Mode of Production, 77,104–105, 106

Nature:
  dialectic of, 19,35–36; and man,
  59–60; natural objects, 52; see also
  Zoology, Scarcity
Naville,P., 20
Necessity:
  dialectical and mechanical, 28; see
  also Determinism, Freedom,
  Marx
Need, 50–53,105–106
Negation, 38
New left, 15,116
Nietzsche,F., 110
Nobel Prize, for Literature, 17

Objectification, 61–63; see also
  Alienation, Reification
Objectivity, and objectivism:
  and analytic reason, 27; and
  dialectical reason, 78; and subject,
  21–22,50
Ontology, 51
Organisation, 89–91
Other-direction, 99–100

Pareto,V., 97
Party, 19,101,104,107
Passivity, 58
Peasantry, 41,59
Philosophy:
  and logocentrism, 45–47; 'moments
  of creation', 17; see also Analytic
  reason, Dialectic, Epistemology,
  Materialism, Ontology
Pledge, 88–89
Plato, 45
Political economy, 78
Positivism, 9,19,21; and marxism,
  32–33; see also Analytic reason,
  Kant
Practico-inert:
  and alienation, 60–61,64; and class-
  being, 73–74; and groups, 82–83;
  and labour, 104; overcoming, 106;
  and series, 67; see also Alienation,

Freedom, Groups, Institution,
  Matter, Praxis
Praxis:
  and alienation, 63–64; constituted,
  107; common, 84–88,92–94; and
  historical materialism, 22–23;
  individual, 43–44,102; in the
  institution, 95; see also Class, Groups,
  History, Practico-inert, Praxis-
  process, Process, Series
Praxis-process, 103
Presence, 45,46,110
Process, 93–94
Progressive-regressive method, 24–25,
  30,47,49
Project:
  and human action, 22; and need, 51;
  and stalinism, 30; see also Praxis,
  Progressive-regressive method
Proletariat, 12,13; and class
  consciousness, 41–42; and dialectic,
  108–110; failure to win power, 23–24;
  in history, 103–109; Lukacs' view of,
  50; and party, 19; revolutionary
  role of, 113; and telos of history, 28;
  universality of, 62; see also Alterity,
  Class, Labour, Revolution
Public opinion, 72

von Ranke,O., 46
Rassemblement Démocratique
  Révolutionnaire, 10
Rationalism, 9
Reason, and history, 15
Reich,W., 113
Reification, 67,69
Reisman,D., The Lonely Crowd, 99
Reciprocity, 42–43,56,69,88; of
  antagonism, 104; mediated, 96
Revolution:
  and dialectical reason, 31; and
  history, 21; and marxism, 20,23;
  and proletariat, 12,104; socialist,
  114–115; see also Communism,
  Proletariat

Robespierre,A., 88
Ruling Class, 99; see also Bourgeoisie

Sartre,J.-P.:
  Baudelaire, 118; Being and
  Nothingness, 9,103; and Critique,
  112; existence, definition of, 95;
  existential psychoanalysis, 119;
  freedom, 12,13; and individualism,
  44; and ontology, 51
  The Communists and the Peace, 13;
  development of ideas, 10–15;
  'Existentialism is a humanism', 103;
  The Family Idiot, 118–120; The
  Ghost of Stalin, 13,14; 'Materialism
  and revolution', 11; Nausea, 9; On a
  Raison de se Révolter, 118; pessimism
  of, 115; recent views of, 116–120;
  Saint Genet: Comédien et Martyr,
  118; Sartre par Lui-Même, 118;
  Search for a Method, 14,17,30;
  'Self portrait at seventy', 102;
  Situations X, 118; The Transcendence
  of the Ego, 9; What is Literature?, 11
Scarcity, 49,53–57; and alienation,
  63; eradication of, 102,105,106;
  and interest, 66; and series, 69; see also
  Series
Series, and seriality, 66–72,81,96–100;
  see also Alterity, Class, Groups,
  Institution, Practico-inert, Praxis
Sociology, and sociologists, 27–28,
  105,113–114
Soviet Union:
  critique of, 41,100–101; cult of
  personality, 100; Sartre's attitude
  to, 10–15,18; see also Stalinism
Spain, 60
Stalin, 19
Stalinism:
  effect on marxism, 18–20,30–31,
  36–37; see also Soviet Union

State, 98–99
Structuralism, 77; see also Marxism
Subject, and subjectivity, 42–43,50–51,
  112
Surplus, 54
Surviving group, 87–88
Sweezy,P., 20
Synthetic totaliser, 107

Technology, 55,56,76; technological
  rationality, 108; see also Machines
Television, 117–118
Telos see History
Temporality, 38,46
Les Temps Modernes, 11,12
Tennis Court Oath, 88
Terror, 88
Things, and human beings, 49–80,
  92,94,103; see also Alienation,
  Matter, Practico-inert, Series
Third world, 24,88
Thompson,E.P., The Making of the
  English Working Class, 112
Totalisation:
  and dialectical reason, 37–38; and
  freedom, 48; and historical
  materialism, 22–23; and logocentrism,
  45–46; and need, 51; and stalinism,
  30; 'without a totaliser', 111; see also
  Dialectic, Praxis

Vietnam, 10,88,115
Violence, 56–57,88–89; see also
  Force

Weber,M., 97,101
Williams,R., 20
Women, 106; see also Domination,
  Family